The Message Boy II

The Message Boy II

JOHN NANT

At time of writing John lived in
South East Queensland Australia.

THE MESSAGE BOY II

iUniverse books may be ordered through booksellers or by contacting:

iUniverse
1663 Liberty Drive
Bloomington, IN 47403
www.iuniverse.com
1-800-Authors (1-800-288-4677)

ISBN: 978-1-5320-5707-6 (sc)
ISBN: 978-1-5320-5708-3 (e)

Library of Congress Control Number: 2018910318

Print information available on the last page.

iUniverse rev. date: 09/20/2018

This book is dedicated to all of those in spirit who come with love & light, help, guidance and healing to all living beings. Also to those friends who help me daily on my journey. May the love & light be with you brighter and stronger than ever before.

John W Nant

Contents

Chapter One

Acknowledgements

First off, thank you to my wife again for persevering with my very different and way out ideals. Also to those who rang me out of the blue, just to pass on a message from the spirit world as an incentive for me to continue on the path that I am on. Thank you all. You all know who you are and have been a great help. On many occasions I would receive a message from spirit about a certain issue which to me seemed way out, and yet, usually within 24 hrs someone would ring me just to verify what I had received from spirit. Amazing. Thank you all again.

And now to thank very much my Guides and Helpers from the spirit world. I do know that my Guides come from the highest realms of love & light. And all my Helpers also. Plus special thanks to the team. Pure Love & Light is the creator, and I am very blessed that I have had sent to me all of those above. Absolutely Amazing Thank you again, Love You All.

John

Hello, Best Wishes and Thank you to those who read my first book THE MESSAGE BOY, and also to those who are reading this book. I have had many people call me to say thank you for writing the message boy exactly as it happened. True words and true life stories. Many people said, once they started reading the book they did not want to put it down until it was finished. It only took around two hours to read it, so most people did read it until it was finished. Funny enough many people woke up during the night and started to read it then. The main remarks re the message boy were "Loved it. Thank you", a little bit short though. But as explained in the beginning, this book was written to explain to the people about the continuation of life after the physical experience. But then on the other hand most people replied, "We knew there was a second book coming by the way it ended".

They also replied that they really loved the true experience stories and would like to hear some more. So here we are THE MESSAGE BOY II. What was surprising to me is that how many people have told me about their spiritual experiences which they had never spoken to anyone about before. Many of them were regarding pets that they'd had and also family pets. The majority of experiences that people had experienced and never told anyone about were family members: mainly parents or grandparents. Some of the people were feeling them around or sensing them; sometimes they would actually see a spirit being and knew who they were. With the animals on most occasions, the people could feel them and sometimes even feel them walking or sleeping on their bed, where they used to when in the physical. As explained in the Message Boy, all stories and experiences were 100% the truth and the same goes for this book THE MESSAGE BOY II.

The first part of this book up to messages from my guides from the spirit realm, are all my own experiences. The second part of this book is relayed messages and stories from my spirit guides which I have been asked to write. No names are mentioned but all stories and situations are as they actually happened. Every now and again somebody would say to me "What a load of rubbish", or else will just laugh with a very cynical laugh of nonbelief. As I always say to them, you are allowed to believe in whatever you want, just because it has never happened to you, there is really no need to disbelieve someone else's true life experiences. Many things are possible in life. Also by the way, and this is including myself, I have never met anyone who knows everything there is to know about everything in life. But I will say, I have met a few who think that they do. What is funny though, is that most of those people who actually think they know everything, know the least. I am sure many of these people just like arguing, also a little put out that someone else knows or has experienced something that they really do not or have not.

Short Stories Of Actual Experiences

A short while ago a lady came to see me regarding being able to be in touch with her mother. Straight away there was a message from her mother saying that she is in the kitchen with her daughter many times, especially when she is cooking her husband's favourite meal which happens to be a special pie. With this the lady started to laugh and replied. It was my mother who started off the liking of the pie in the first place, spoiling my husband. The lady in the room then asked if her mother had anything else to say. Yes was the reply, you still cannot cook very good. With this remark the lady burst into tears, then lots of laughter, "that's my mother for sure, she was an excellent cook and was always telling me that I am not a very good cook, and that I should learn more". Not only that, I cooked the special pie last week and burnt it. I also felt my mother was in the room then. I replied, Yes your mother was, and she is saying that she always stands on your left side when you are cooking and often strokes your hair (your mum is asking is that okay for her to do that?) "Yes definitely okay" said the lady. "It makes me feel good and reminds me of her". I loved her dearly and we were great friends. When I receive messages like that it makes me feel very blessed to be able to pass them on.

A while ago I was having a mediumship night with twenty people. I looked at a lady with a blue top on and said, "A man called Fred is saying that he was your husband and he likes the colour that you just painted your lounge". He then said he was not fussed about the colour of the dining room he thought it might of looked better with your first choice of colour. The lady in blue replied "you can talk to him just like that?" I replied, "Yes, just like that. "Wow" she said, "Fred was my husband and he passed away ten years ago, also he was a painter. I got the lounge painted last week and yesterday the dining room. When I got home from work last night the painters had just finished the dining room. I really didn't like it, and I think I shall get the painters to paint it again with my first choice of colour. I shouldn't have changed my mind at the last moment." I then said to the lady "Fred just said your choice, a good idea though. He still loves you dearly and that you always were the love of his life, and still is apart from the creator. Also by the way he was with his family and please do not worry about him as he is home, and it is truly magnificent where he is. Better than your best dream you've ever had by a million times plus, Love Fred."

I then looked at a lady with a dark coloured jacket and then said. "I just received a message for you and the lady sitting next door to you. Apparently you are both sisters and have race horses". "Yes that's right" was the reply. Well, I then gave them a message from spirit saying "You have two young race horses and that you believe that they are the ones that are going to be winners and make you a lot of money". "That's right the lady said that is what we believe and we were also told that two horses are going to be great". "Well the gentleman in spirit just said not quite correct, not those two but the next two. You have a young foal and also another ready to be born". The lady looked at me in disgust. "No its the two we already have. We do have a young horse and another one coming, you are correct in that department and also by the way who is giving you this information". I then replied "He said he is your uncle the horse trainer. The lady looking a little shocked then replied. Well if he said so that will be true because he was one of the best horse trainers in Australia and he departed eighteen months ago. I wish we had not come here tonight now". The room went very quiet. I then passed on the message. "All he was trying to do was to save you a lot of money time and effort and please, the next two will be the best that you have ever had. Thank You for listening Love and Light, Uncle."

I then turned to a lady with a pink top. "There is a man here in spirit called Alf, he said that he was your husband and he said that you are looking at buying a new car. You keep looking at a white one and also a red one. He then said that you like the red one the most, but the white one is better mechanically. The red one will last five months and the motor will cost you a lot of money to fix." "That would be right" the lady said. "He was my husband and passed away fifteen years ago. Not only that, he was a motor mechanic and knowing him he would have checked out both cars because he was very good at what he did. I also always wanted a sports car and the red one is a two door sports. But never mind I will go with his advice and get the white one. It's a good car but it's a four door saloon." The reply from the husband was, "Your choice but a good idea. I love you dearly, always did and always will. Love and Light Alf, and also by the way, it is magnificent here. Please do not worry about me and please enjoy your new car."

I then turned to a Japanese lady and saw a very big sumo wrestler standing in front of her in spirit. I then explained to her what I was seeing and said that he was a guardian. "Also his name is Somo, the sumo wrestler and was a family member." The Japanese lady replied. "I don't know maybe a cousin" but that she did not know many of her family relatives anyway. After a few more messages from people that she did know, said "thank you I will ask my mother tonight". The next morning the Japanese lady booked in for a one on one session. When she arrived the first words to me were Somo the sumo wrestler was my uncle and he was one of Japan's top wrestlers.

A few months ago a gentleman came into my healing room and asked if I would know how to help him and his sister make their mothers life a little more comfortable. Their mother was in a nursing home and couldn't remember who he was. He said that his mother always recognised his sister but used to ask him, "Who are you? When he told her who he was she did not even answer. All of a sudden on a spiritual level, his mother came through and asked me to please explain to her son that there is nothing that either of them can do to ease the pain. She is ready to leave and go home. I then repeated his mother's words to the gentleman and also said to him "Your mother just asked for you to ring the rest of the family to please explain, that it would be of benefit to all if you went and saw her as soon as possible." The gentleman replied, "I will ring the family and let them know but I don't know where they all live. We have not had a family gathering for at least fifteen years." The gentleman's mother then said spiritually to me, please ask my son to call his sister because she knows where they all live. This particular day was a Tuesday. He then said I am busy this weekend but I shall go and see her the following weekend. I then repeated the words his mother had just said. "AS SOON AS POSSIBLE."

On the Friday of that same week I came across the same gentleman at a shopping centre, he came over to me and explained that he had phoned everybody in the family; he had changed his mind and was going to visit his mother tomorrow. "It is a three and a half hour drive and we will see what happens". Two weeks went by and then I saw him at a local market. "John" he called out, "can

I please give you a hug?" I looked at him and said, warily "Okay why?" "Well," he replied "I went to see my mum, as I explained to you, on the Saturday. On the Sunday morning our whole family turned up from all around different parts of Australia. That is the first time that we have all met together for fifteen years. We all had a lot to say and lots of laughter. And then Mum passed away Sunday night." With tears in both of our eyes he said "Thank you, I thought I would just let you know". Its moments like that I feel very blessed, to be able to be a part of what had just happened. Love and Light to you all.

A few weeks ago I was in North Queensland Australia, at a reasonable size town by the Great Barrier Reef. A friend of mine had organised an evening for a few people and myself to have an evening with spirit night. The first lady I talked to said straight away, "I want proof!" I replied "Do you believe in life after the physical body?" "I would like to" was the reply, "but nobody has ever shown me proof." I replied, "I shall do my best, but I can only give you what I receive." "Okay I will listen, we'll see." the lady replied. The next moment her mother gave me a message about her daughter saying, she always was a very sceptical person and also a total know all! A whole lot more information I passed on to the lady. As the information stopped for a moment, I asked the lady if she could relate to any of the messages. She just looked at me and said "what else?" With this the mother in spirit replied. "Please explain to my daughter what I said first up about being sceptical and a know all." So I did. With this the other people in the class smiled to themselves and the lady just looked at me smiled and then replied, "That's my mum for sure, because that's what she always used to say to me. "Stop being a know all because you are not." After a few tears were shed her mother then told her how much she loved her and who she was with in spirit. I then passed a message on from one of her favourite grandparents. Then to the surprise of all the people in the class, the lady in question looked at me and said "I want what you've got and I want to be able to do what you do". I then looked at the lady and replied. "You cannot have what I have got, because I will not give it to you". "Why not?" was the reply from the lady and also in a very aggressive manner. I then replied:

"No 1. What I have is mine.
No 2. I am not giving it away.
No 3. You might be able to do what I can do if you are prepared to learn, I can teach you, or show you what I know, if you are interested"

"No" was the reply, "I want what you have got and I want it now!" With this another lady from the group stood up and then a gentleman also. Both then said "Please, you can learn about what is happening here tonight, but it just does not happen instantly because you want it to." The lady who this story is about just replied "Never did believe in it anyway" and with this hardly spoke a word for the rest of the night. Everyone else in the group that night passed on messages from spirit to each other and it ended up an amazing night.

The next day I was having a one on one session with another lady who was also at the evening group the night before. She explained what had come to her during that evening. It was explained to her by her spirit guides that it was of benefit not to ask that night about a certain lady who was in spirit. When the lady mentioned this, I looked at the seat beside her and said, "Was the lady that you were wanting to ask about, around twenty five years old and has long dark hair?" "Yes" was the reply, "is she here?" "Yes, she is actually sitting in the chair beside you has a great big smile and said thank you for thinking of her, also thank you for sending her healing while she was in hospital." With this the lady in the physical broke down and cried for quite a while. When the tears stopped flowing, the lady said I used to send her healing every day and wondered why someone who was so young and such a beautiful person could be that sick, and also why the healing that I used to send her everyday did not work. When the extra tears dried up a message from the lady in spirit said "The healing did work. But please remember it was my time to go home. Consciously it wasn't, but on a soul spiritual level it was. It is written before we even arrive on the earth plane, what year, time and date we depart the earth plane and return home to the highest realms of Love and Light." The twenty five year old in spirit then relayed many messages to her physical friend sitting in front of me. That session ended with many other family members in spirit coming through with messages.

MESSAGES FROM SPIRIT FOR MYSELF

My wife and I own a 40 ft yacht. Every year it is to come out of the water so that the hull can be cleaned & polished, also new antifouling paint on the bottom of the hull to stop the plant life growing on it while sitting in the water. It was nearing the time for all of this to happen, I went to ring up the boat yard and make a booking for a week ahead. A message came from my spirit guides, please wait for another three and a half weeks. So listening to the message I never rang the boat yard. Well within a few days it started to rain, and guess what? It rained for three weeks. I received another message from my spirit guides with the exact dates that would be most beneficial for me to take the yacht out of the water and repaint the bottom. With this I booked the boat yard. The rain stopped the day before I started, and then started raining again the day I put it back in the water. I was very grateful as most people would realise that you do not paint the bottom of your boat when it is raining. It saved me a lot of money.

When I wrote The Message Boy,

my wife and I were living on the Gold Coast Queensland Australia. My wife was working on the Sunshine Coast a two hour drive north. After living there on the Gold Coast, my wife suggested, how about we sail north one hundred miles and live a lot closer to her work. I replied, Not really I have built up a good clientele here. About a month later I had a vision of us living on the yacht on the Sunshine Coast, also in the vision I had shop as a healing room at the marina. That's strange I thought. I really had no intention of moving. When I told my wife that night, she laughed, so have I. Well we thought about it some more and I came up with the idea, "What say we look at moving in three to four months' time?" I then received a message from my spirit guides, "Please move up north in four to five weeks' time". "No way", I replied, "not yet". "Please trust" were the words I received from spirit, "please do and you shall see why". As long as we have moved by a certain date all will be well, please trust. Well the universe certainly has a way of organising. Everybody stopped coming to see me, so I had no clients booked at all for the next few weeks. So anyway the next weekend, my wife and I drove a hundred miles north to the Sunshine Coast to have a look at the marina. Both of us agreed, "Sounds good, and looks good, let's give it a try". During the following week I rang the marina office to try to get a marina berth as I was told we would be very lucky to get one, as they are usually fully booked. The marina manager said "Yes, you can have a berth for that size yacht and you are very lucky, the boat that was there is going up north in one weeks' time. How long do you wish to be here?" "At least a year" I replied. "Perfect," the manager said "it's yours". So up to the Sunshine Coast we came.

The next day after arriving I went for a walk around the marina shopping complex looking to see if there was an empty shop, which I had seen in my vision. Well I didn't find it and also there were no empty shops, they were all full and seemed busy. I then asked my guides "What's up! What is the story getting me up here at this time?" I received a short message back from spirit "PLEASE TRUST". Two weeks later a candle shop closed down and funnily enough, it was the shop that I had seen in my vision. I then went straight to the centre management, checked the shop out, and the next day with a mutual agreement on time and price I signed a lease. As I was signing the lease, the manager of the complex said, "You are very lucky, there is someone else wanting this shop and I do know that they shall not be very happy. But we do not have a shop here that does what you do so good luck". I walked away, went down to the yacht and thanked my spirit guides very much. If we had not moved when we did, I would not have been there when the shop became available. At the time of writing this story I have been in this shop two years.

More Stories

Every now and again I have someone come into the shop to tell me that I am a bad man and a heathen, because they think that there is no way I could speak to those who have passed. Most of them are so brainwashed about life they actually have no idea about how life is after the physical. The message that I receive from my spirit guides, who by the way are pure love & light, is please be patient with people with that attitude. All it is, is that they are slightly misguided by those who actually do not really know what is. I receive confirmation on that subject many times from those who have passed on to the realms of Love and Light. Also as I have already written before, many people in spirit just love to be able to pass a message to their loved ones and friends, who are still physical on the earth plane.

On many occasions during a mediumship session those in spirit have me in fits of laughter. Especially when they pass on a message to the person in front of me about the ideals and beliefs that they had held dearly in their physical life, only to find out, that none of it, or most of the beliefs were not so. That particular story happens a lot. Many of those now in spirit pass on messages to me how they had been so strict on people and family members about certain values and beliefs. Once home to the light they had been shown the truth about what really is. Most of those in spirit who were like that in their values and beliefs explain that is how they were taught, and how many untruths were spread all around the world. It is quite ironic that those who thought they knew all about life and also life after the physical actually knew the least. Just repeating what I have written before:

EVERYBODY GOES HOME, and that is, EVERYBODY GOES HOME no one is excluded.

There are many myths about life after the physical and what I have been told by many who have passed into the light, and also by my guides from the light say the same thing "MYTHS, EVERYBODY GOES HOME."

A while ago my wife and I were out having breakfast at a restaurant coffee shop. I received a message from spirit if I would please give one of my business cards to a lady sitting at the table beside us.

After much hesitation I received the words "Please trust, all is well". Just as the lady and her partner were about to leave, I leaned over and explained to the gentleman what I do, and would it be alright to give one of my business cards to the lady. He looked at me with a look of total confusion and then shrugged his shoulders. He then looked at the lady in question, and as he was about to ask, the lady said "Yes that would be great thank you I know what it is all about". They both stood up and left with a big smile on her face. Apparently her mother had passed away over a week and a half ago and there was a message for her daughter. I am happy that situation doesn't happen too frequently. But when it does, it always work's out perfect in the end. There are so many people who would just like to know if their loved ones are okay once they have passed over.

Several large cruise ships call into where we live, so I have a few people call into see me each time these ships anchor. Even some of the crew have called in for messages from spirit having been recommended by their guests. A short while ago a lady came to see me regarding any messages from her husband. The lady explained that she had been to many mediums before but her husband never came through. Other family members, yes, but not her husband. Before the lady had finished her story her husband came through and kept repeating. "It was not her fault and to please stop blaming herself". The lady started crying profusely, "I always thought it was me" she said. "No, not at all" were the words from her husband. Many different circumstances were happening at that time. He lost his job, had trouble finding another, had a wife and four children, a mortgage to pay and had used up all of their savings. The pressure had got to him and therefore, could not handle it anymore. The lady then said, that is exactly what happened, but she blamed herself for telling him all the time to go and get a job. When the tears slowly dried, she asked me if there were any other messages regarding confirmation. Her husband replied, "How's this". I am with my four mates who passed over one week after I did." The lady then asked, what were their names? I then gave her four names. "You've got to be kidding, those four passed in a car accident one week after he did WOW". The husband then replied. "We were all in spirit sitting on the bonnet of their favourite V8 SUPER CAR driver's car at the last well known motor racing event. With this the lady burst into tears again, saying that the five of them used to go to every V8 super car race there was. A few moments later the last words from her husband were, that he loved her and the children very much and to "please, please, please, stop blaming yourself", it was not her fault. After a lot of tears and face wipes, the lady stood up and said "Thank you that was him for sure, even some of the sayings were his favourites". I then asked her to please look in the mirror as she looked ten years younger. She did so, looked and smiled, some of my wrinkles in my face have gone, "Thank you again." This lady had been holding the guilt for four and a half years. When she walked out the door I looked at the difference in her, and said to life itself, "Thank you. Absolutely Magnificent!" It's moments like that, which makes me feel very blessed, and also gives me the incentive to continue.

In my previous book, The Message Boy, some of the stories were about misguided and confused spirit. Over the last nine years, many people who are light workers have been helping those in spirit who were lost, confused or too scared to return home. Thousands upon thousands have been returning home daily. At this time of writing all have returned home; there are no lost souls wandering around this plane and others anymore. Everybody has gone home, and also everybody who is in the physical now spiritually know where to go, and all return home instantly. There are a few who question this, but if those who do question this could talk to spirit and ask their spirit guides, it shall be explained to them, "THAT IS SO".

A short while ago I was sitting in a coffee shop and happened to get introduced to an English couple on holiday. After a conversation on what we all did for a living, the English lady asked me if I could pick up any information on a gentleman that they

had met in a different part of Australia.
We were on the east coast of Australia
the lady said, and the gentleman in
question lived in Perth, which is on the
opposite side of Australia to where we
are now. The lady then explained that
they had been staying with a friend in
Perth the month before. I was then able
to tune into the gentleman in Perth and
received some interesting information.
I then explained to the lady that the
gentleman in question is actually the
brother of your male companion sitting
right here beside you. With this the lady
burst out laughing, and replied to her
friend. "I told you so, but you did not
believe me". Her male companion sitting
beside me said impossible. I only have

one brother and he lives in England and definitely not here. "Well, I replied, "not so, he is your brother from your father". After a long discussion, the lady said to her partner. "He looks just like you and I was sure that he was a member of your family". About five months later I was speaking to the couple from England and the gentleman just said out of the blue "HEY, by the way, the man in Perth probably was my brother, because my Dad did have a son out of wedlock, he did not know where he was, but had heard that his son had gone to live somewhere in Australia". Anyway, it was noted after a while that it was his brother in Perth. The Universe works in many amazing ways. The people in this story all met in Perth while on holiday and were introduced to each other by a friend. (SMALL WORLD or WHAT)

A lady came to see me, asking about her pet dog which had just passed away. The lady was asking what happens to people's pets and do they go to heaven? "Yes they do", I replied, "they all go to a realm of pure love & light, and your dog is there. Also he is with your Mother and Grandmother. Happy as, and asked me to say thank you for your love that you gave him". He was very happy with you, and is also extremely happy where he is now. As the lady started to cry a whole lot of animals came into the room and sat around her. I then explained to her, there is a small horse, a big boxer dog, two other small dogs, a black and white cat, plus a ginger cat, a rabbit, a guinea pig, and some birds. With this the lady smiled choked up with tears and replied. "I was raised on a farm when I was a little girl. The horse was mine, the boxer was my Mum and Dads, the cats, rabbits, guinea pigs, and the birds that you are describing all belonged to the whole family. We had lots of pets". I then explained to her that there was a small brown and white dog sitting in front of her looking up at her just staring. "That's my dog that passed last week. Thank you, Thank you". I then replied, "It keeps putting its right foot on your leg". "That's what it did when it was seeking attention", the lady replied. "WOW. Exactly spot on totally".

Sometimes, but not very often, there may be only two or three messages for someone. Usually that person never had many friends, or did not know their family. But what messages do come through seem to be very important to that person. A few weeks ago a person came to see me who had no idea who his maternal / paternal parents were. He knew that he was adopted, but was never told who his real parents were. Apparently the foster parents knew the mother, but still never told the man sitting in front of me. This whole story was very different to other circumstances that I have had before. A man came through from spirit explaining that he was the man's Grandfather, he also said that the man's father was still alive in the physical but lived in a different country. Also that he had done so for a long time. The Grandfather did not say the name or the whereabouts of the real father, due to many unforeseen circumstances that would evolve by finding out the truth. The man sitting in front of me just said, "That's okay I can realise the complications that could arise, and anyway, I love my father who raised me very much and would not choose to hurt him in any way". The Grandfather of his mother also came through with a message, and said that he had met his real mother when he was little, but was explained to him at that time that she was an auntie. The Grandfather then went on to explain that his real mother was now in spirit. The gentleman in front of me sitting was not upset or worried in anyway. He just said to me, is my real mother here in spirit today? At that time my spirit guide explained, yes that she was, and was he interested in a message from his maternal mother? The gentleman replied, "No worries, please continue." The real mother came through with a message of love & light, and then went on to explain about the circumstances at the time of birth. Then she went on to explain that it also was a karmic retribution from a life time before. The gentleman sitting in front of me just smiled and replied, I thought that might have been the story, because a clairvoyant lady had said to him many years before that his family life was karmic. He then repeated that he loved his parents, all of them. And all were forgiven. This story to me was quite amazing, and what a beautiful soul sitting in front of me also. Love and Light to all.

A few months ago a lady came to see me to check if there was a negative energy around her. Everywhere she went, the lady felt there was some spirit following her, even while she was watching TV. I then explained to the lady that there was nobody in spirit who had passed over with her that was negative. There were family members and her guides but they were all from the light. I was then shown that a lady from her work was spiritually beside her. I then explained to her what this work colleague looked like. All of a sudden the lady in my room said in a panic, that woman from work is a horrible person and picks on everybody at work. Please get her out of here and to stay away from me. I then asked through my guides what the lady in spirit doing here? My guides explained to me it was a spiritual energy of distaste, distrust and anger which had been directed at my client, simply because my client stood up to this angry lady from work more than the others did. Just then a few others spiritually came into my healing room. When I explained to my client what and who I was seeing, my client said, "They are the people from my work but they are all nice people, they all have trouble with the angry lady also." I then, through my guides asked the new arrivals "what was the story?" They all explained about the angry lady. So with this I said to the angry lady, "WHATS UP with you and why are you so angry and annoyed with everyone?" The reply from the angry lady was, "I don't like anyone from work because they don't like me, also I don't like the work but I need the money". I then passed a few messages to her from the others in the room, and also from her past family members in spirit from the light. After my messages to the angry lady she put her nose in the air and replied "you can all get lost" and then disappeared. My client just looked at me and said you've got to be kidding, is this a game or what?" "No game" I explained, "that is how life is sometimes". I then said to my client, "I received a message myself from my guides of pure love & light, for you to see what happens at work over the next few days". About a week and a half later I received a phone call from my client, to say that the angry lady just threw her job in and just left. "Also everybody at work is so much happier, and the workplace has now a great feeling to it. As strange as it all seemed, I would just like to say, thank you from myself and all of my workmates."

Many people come to see me

explaining that they feel someone in spirit is hanging around them. I explain to them all, that if spirit from the light is with them, they never feel bothered or threatened, and that most of the time it is an energy that has been projected on them by someone else. Life is amazing and to think that we only know a very small part of it. I still get people who think that the planet earth has the only living beings in the whole universe. Well guess what? That is not so. Please remember what you put out verbally, goes out into the universe, you put it there, you own it. It's up to you to remove it. There are many people these days, like myself who can help you in that respect. But what is amazing, is what forgiveness does to all.

I have had people who have come into my healing room with that many negative thought forms, they have a stooped posture and look like they're carrying the weight of the world on their shoulders. Nearly every time those people who arrive like that, stop at the front door. Lots of the time I can see what the thought forms are about. My guides remove all of those thought forms in a flash. Most times quicker than I can even blink. Then the people walk into my shop standing upright automatically. Some of the people even say, I feel great at the moment and really I do not feel that it is necessary for me to come inside.

I just look at them and smile, then relay to them what just happened and what I saw. Once they come inside and into the healing room, I then explain to them where the thought forms come from, and who is directing them. Many of these sessions, as just explained, are created by the people they work with, Family, so called friends, or just acquaintances. Often after explaining who, why and where they came from, my client will explain their side of the story and also an explanation of the whole scenario. When these sessions finish, I usually ask my client would they forgive all of those involved. Many times the client does forgive them all, and when they do the energy around them changes completely. Every time my client says "no not forgiving", I receive a phone call usually within two to three weeks asking for another session. Just to repeat, when they do forgive, it is absolutely amazing. The change in themselves and the people involved. On many occasions I receive a phone call to say thank you, because everybody around me is being really nice, WOW, should have done this a long time ago. Also what happens is that those people, who were the main trouble makers or stirrers, usually depart and move somewhere else. Now and again the main trouble maker of the situation has been my client. Once explained and defused they realise it was them, and they change quite dramatically.

Sometimes even get a new job, new friends, or a new partner.

Not too long ago a lady asked me if I could find out what was causing her middle back discomfort. "I keep getting these jabbing pains. Don't know why, I have been to see others about it" she said, "but they all say, I must have twisted myself lifting something, or twisted myself in bed while I was asleep". "Well" I replied, "please stand up and turn around". As I went to place my hand on her back, I noticed a spiritual knife had been placed in the exact part of the back which was giving her the problem. I then tuned into the back scenario, "which lady at work does not like you and is very jealous of you?" "Oh," she replied that sounds like ----------- I work with her every day and we always end up having an argument". I then said to her, "what I am getting is that you are qualified and the other particular lady is not. Also the knife in your back belongs to her. Are you friends or would you rather the knife comes out? Because if I pull it out it shall be taken by the light and you will see a very big difference in her personality tomorrow". She replied "please pull it out I am sick and tired of her nonsense". With that, I put my hand around the handle of the spiritual knife that I could see and pulled it out. I just saw a very bright light in a flash and the knife was gone. "WOW", stated my client, I could feel it come out and now my back is so much better, not great, but a lot better. Is it alright to be able to do such a thing as pull it out?" asked my client. I then explained to her that it was not karmic and to please remember it is a spiritual story and the lady in question who placed the knife, consciously has no idea of what has happened. Please remember the old sayings:

A CERTAIN PERSON IS A
PAIN IN THE NECK
HE OR SHE DRIVES ME CRAZY
HE OR SHE GIVES ME
A HEADACHE
HE OR SHE IS A PAIN
IN THE BUTT

There are many sayings like these and they have been around for hundreds of years. My client then sat down and started to explain more about her work situation and also how annoying the other lady was. Once she had finished explaining to me all about her work and the people whom she had spent five days a week with, I then asked her to please stand up and walk around the room. This the lady did, then just stared at me and replied, "how did all that happen? It all seems so way out and strange. But I have no pain at all and look how free and flexible I am. Amazing, thank you". Three days later, the lady client called me to say that the other lady in question, handed in her notice at work and was leaving. (P.S. I usually defuse one of these situations around every two months).

A short while ago I received a phone call from a person who lived one thousand kilometres away. This Lady explained to me how a spirit of some sort was in her house and invading her space, plus her dog would not go into her house while this spirit was there. The lady who phoned explained to me how she can see and talk to the spirit world also, but had never come across anything like this energy ever before. The spirit kept telling the lady that she was a fool. The lady also said this wayward spirit kept saying that she was a Hawaiian princess. I then received a message from my spirit guides that the spirit being was definitely not a Hawaiian princess, but was the spirit of a very drug overdosed human. I then explained this to my client, and then the spirit said a few swear words and kept saying that she was a Hawaiian princess, and that the lady who owns the house is a fool. The lady replied to the spirit, "Get out of my house!" but to no avail. So I asked one of my warrior guides from the light to please remove the drug overdosed spirit. Within a couple of seconds, the lady who owned the house said, "WHAT HAPPENED?" I just saw a big flash of light and the spirit disappeared, also my dog just came back into the house. WOW amazing, just like that. The message that I received from my spirit guides, was that a lady from another country who was staying in that town had totally lost herself in a drug induced state and had split herself. I heard a couple of weeks later that all was well with the lady and her dog. That experience was a first for me, regarding the fragmentation of a spirit through drugs.

GREAT BENEFITS

A week ago I was on the internet looking at sailing times and prices for the New Zealand inter-island ferry service. Also I was looking at prices and availabilities on motels in the top end of the South Island, as my wife and I were looking to go there for Xmas holidays. North Island first and then the South Island to Kaikura and Christchurch for a week. As I was looking, I received a vision of the Kaikura coastline. Very dark, grey like heavy rain, also very rough seas with breaking waves. So to me, no trip to the South Island forget it another time will be okay. One week later a big earthquake happened at Kaikura and all the road and rail lines had collapsed. Many of them had tons of landslides on top of them "WOW". As I wrote in my first book The Message Boy please be aware. Many people have these sorts of visions and take no notice of them. My vision just saved my wife and I a great big hassle and also a lot of money.

Many people ask me if I can turn off from receiving messages, or do I get bombarded with them all the time? My guides are from the highest realms of love & light and they do not bombard me with messages. But the messages that

I do receive, always seem to come out at the exact moment to help me with a certain situation that might be arising, that I consciously do not know about. Whether the messages are directly for me or for others, I am truly thankful for those messages. To answer anyone else who is wondering, YES, I can tune them out if I choose to. As I have stated many times before my spirit guides are from a realm of pure love & light and therefore only give me messages at an appropriate time, and all messages come with love & light.

I have sat in many rooms with people receiving messages from spirit. Some of these people receive their messages very differently to myself. For example some will be guided to say over on the left of the room, 2nd or 3rd row back a person by the name of Bill would like to pass on a message. Who in this corner knows someone named Bill in spirit. Usually someone puts their hand up and sometimes more than one. My guides come through very different, they just say "to the lady in the front row with a pink top, a man called Bill said he was your husband and would like to pass a message to you regarding you getting a new car. Is that alright with you?" Every time I trust in this sort of message it has been correct. Now and again someone will say "no not me, my husband's name was William not Bill!" Normally when this happens in a group session the rest of the people seem to smile and chuckle to each other. Sometimes doing this type of work I am sure some people just try to test you. Now and again I do say to people, "Are you trying to test me, or trying to prove me wrong?" Most of them say no not really, "why do you ask?" I usually just smile because my guides tell me so and sometimes have already explained to me before the actual happening. Well I am a message boy, so I call myself, and I do trust what I receive. Now and again if I do pass on a message which makes people query, it is usually something that they have forgotten. Most times, a short while after, they call out "Got it!" On many occasions people say to me, you must have seen many amazing circumstances while doing this type of work? My usual reply is yes, nearly every week in fact. On many occasions people ask for one of my favourite experiences. So here is one of them. Many years ago I went to a small seminar in Brisbane Queensland, Australia. The speaker was the founder of a method of kinesiology named "Three In One" Concept. Halfway through the morning, this particular gentleman (who was by the way a GENTLEMAN) from America, asked if there was anyone in the room who could not read. One gentleman put his hand up and replied never have been able to. "My mother has spent thousands of dollars on speech therapy, but I still cannot read properly".

The lecturer asked the forty five year old gentleman if he would be willing to stand up in front of fifty people and try to read. With this the forty five year old walked up on to the stage in front of the people and said "WHY NOT, nothing to lose". As he was given a book he shrugged his shoulders and then looked very nervous. He started to read and could manage a few words slowly, then stop and stammer doing this throughout the whole page. When asked to read the page backwards, he did so very slowly but no stammering. With this the lecturer explained how some letters and numbers trigger of a stress response; also reading backwards was not normal. So then the lecturer found out what letters of the alphabet were stress triggers. By holding the man's head and hand and using his method of kinesiology, all letters of stress were shown and why. With a certain method of defusing these letters, it came to the attention that the man had been told off many times when trying to learn to read or to say the alphabet. Most of this was when he was a young boy growing up. After ten minutes of defusing, the gentleman could say the alphabet just as well as everyone else. The lecturer then handed the man the book again and asked him to read the same page as before. This the gentleman did, he read the page from top to bottom and then from the bottom to the top, then another page from top to bottom and then a third page, then burst out crying. With this emotion there were fifty people with tears running down their faces. Here was this forty five year old six foot biker gentleman in his leather jacket standing in front of fifty people reading perfectly for the first time in his life. With tears running down my face I just thought to myself how magnificent was that. "THANK YOU GORDEN." That is one story I tell, and there are many more amazing stories and gifts that I have seen and been part of. "WOW", "Beautiful". I do live in 'WOW' mode quite often.

Every now and again a client comes to me who is a clairvoyant, a medium or both 'so they say'. It is very strange or amazing how the universe works. We do get tested many times. Some of the clairvoyants tell me straight away and for others, it's like a secret, 'try and catch me if you can' sort of game. The funny part about it all, is my spirit guides explain to me most of the time who and what they are before they even arrive. Most of the time, the ones who do not say anything are very good at what they do. We usually go through the whole session and then they say, thank you and by the way I have some messages from spirit for you if you are interested. I always say yes thank you please go ahead. The majority are very accurate. Most times with these people who are very good we end up talking for quite some time. I do enjoy the company of like-minded people. Now those who tell me how good they are, usually are the opposite. I normally just smile and do not say very much. Once you have met or have sat in a room with very good ones, you're inclined to be a little critical of the others. You know straight away how they are. I find that many of the below average ones charge their clients a reasonable amount, but make up stories as they go. It is a shame that the percentage of very good ones is not that high. There are a few who have come to me asking about the best way to run classes and evening with spirit nights. Myself, to them I say little, for the simple reason. Good clairvoyants and mediums do not need to ask anybody. Now, many clairvoyants are not good mediums, and also many mediums are not good clairvoyants. A small amount of very good ones can do both. A clairvoyant generally can see what the future entails for their client. A spirit medium channels messages and information from the spirit realm. The reason I call myself the message boy is just that, no clairvoyant information. Just messages and information from spirit guides and others in spirit. I can see spirit and also talk to many animals. If there is any information regarding the future to my clients, it comes from their loved ones in spirit, or from their spirit guides. That is if they choose to accept. LOVE AND LIGHT.

ANIMALS

A few weeks ago a lady rang me regarding her dog. Apparently her two dogs have always joined the family on the back balcony of their two storey house. This particular night the family and friends had a barbeque on the balcony of their house and both dogs were happily playing and mixing with them all. When the party was finished the guests went home and the family went inside, also the two dogs went downstairs to where they usually sleep. The next night when the lady arrived home from work, her four sons explained to her that the big dog is acting strange. It won't go upstairs to the balcony, and when any of them tried to go near it, or approach it in any way, it just cowered down and started to panic. The lady asked me if I could tune into the dog and find out what had happened. I tuned into the dog plus the situation. The message I received was that later on during the same night after the party, some male had climbed the fence and was trying to break into her house. The big dog had run up the stairs to chase away the intruder, but the intruder kicked the dog very hard, the dog was then frightened of everyone. But not only that the intruder was a friend of a friend of theirs. No names came to me but it was definitely someone they knew. That was why the dog did not bark. After explaining to the lady, I then said to her, the dog will show you who it was the next time the male comes around. Three weeks' later the lady rang to say she knew who it was, because a certain person who was always coming to their house just stopped coming. No phone calls, no explanation. I then explained to her that I received no names but that she was close with her presumptions. I then spoke to the dog, and now the dog goes back up the stairs and plays with the family on the back balcony. I have never had any names given to me regarding that incident, but I did receive a message.

What that intruder did that night to the dog has been given back to him big time.

My wife and I live on a yacht at a marina. There are many nights that we hear big fish splashing around and banging into the side of the yacht. Most of the time the noise comes from big fish chasing the small ones. Sometimes the bang on the hull is so noisy it wakes us up, on many occasions I have jumped out of bed and gone outside to see what is going on, only to see a dolphin swimming around the yacht. Now and again I can talk to it and sometimes it gives me messages regarding my work and personal information. Every morning as we climb off the yacht and on to the marina jetty there would be at least one hundred fish swim to the surface right beside where we stand. Some of these fish would be up to fifteen inches in length. One particular day I knelt down on the jetty pontoon and asked the fish if they would like something to eat, and would they eat it out of my hand. "TRY US" was the reply, so I got a slice of bread and held it in the water, and no, they wouldn't take it. The next moment I received, "Let it go and see what happens". So I did. Well it was on for young and old, one big feeding frenzy. I went to stand up and walk away, then received another message. We will eat it out of your hand tomorrow. So the next morning they were all waiting for me at the side of the yacht. I looked at them all then knelt down. I then received a message, "please hold the bread and we will eat it out of your hand", and that they did, no feeding frenzy, no lost or bitten fingers. "Try tomorrow" I received, so the next morning I held the bread in the water, all the fish were there but not eating. Then I received not yet please wait. So with this I held the food in the water they all swam around it but not one fish touched it. I said to them, "are you playing games with me or what?" "No" was the reply. A larger fish came up to the food and took a bite, "now we all will" and that they did. It was a very interesting scenario. Nowadays they just say "hold it" or "throw it, we want to play" and they do.

Now the reason that I have put this story in the book is for those who choose to remember. On a spiritual level you can talk to anything that chooses to talk to you. Please remember, EVERYTHING is ENERGY.

At the beginning of 2016 where I have my shop at Mooloolaba, Sunshine Coast Queensland Australia, there used to be an open market every Friday. One of these Friday's one of the market stall holders came into my shop in a bit of a panic. John could you please come and have a look and help a pigeon, it cannot fly and will not move. So I went along with her and here was this pigeon bird with one wing hanging down and could hardly walk. I went and sat on the step beside it and asked it spiritually "What's up?" A broken wing and was in shock was what I received. I placed my hand about nine inches above the pigeon, and went to ask the Universe for Healing from the highest realms of love & light for the bird, and a flash of pure bright white light just surrounded the pigeon. In an instant the broken wing went back into place, the bird jumped up on to the next step, said thank you and then flew away. "WOW" was the reply from the lady, and a few others watching. The lady who came into my shop said "amazing, but I knew you could do It because I had a dream last night that you did and we all saw". "Well", I replied, "please thank the love & light of all there is, not me and I went back to my shop". Funny part about it, I had never met this lady before. Later on that afternoon I went for a walk around the market. I stopped at the ladies stall just to say hello, when she said that the pigeon had been back to her stall many times during the day. Just at that time the pigeon flew up beside me and said "thank you, watch this". So the lady and I did. The pigeon landed on the bottom step then jumped up five steps one at a time, then flew up to the top of the rails around the market, "ALL FIXED. See you around". I used to see this pigeon nearly every week and quite often it would have a message for me from spirit. LOVE AND LIGHT to you all.

Another dog story. A few months ago while I was in North Queensland a lady rang to ask if I could find out why her two dogs would not go outside to the back of the house anymore. I just happened to be in her area at that time, so I ended up going around to her house. Well the two dogs raced up to me, did everything that I asked them to do, we were like long lost friends. I sat down and then tuned into what was happening. I then explained to the lady that there was a very dangerous snake, at the back of the house in the long grass and had been there for three to four weeks. The lady replied, that's how long it has been since they have gone out the back and played. I also received that the snake will be there for one more day, and then move on. Also to please explain to her husband, it would be of benefit not to go looking for it. Spiritually the big dog said thank you it is a big dangerous snake, a taipan in fact, thank you again I am looking forward to playing out the back of the house again with my friend. How the other dog stayed as its friend would be anyone's guess. The friend as the big dog called it was only about eight inches high and about fourteen inches long. The big dog used to jump on it, chew its ear and wait for the response. Then they would play fight for five minutes, and make up afterwards. Puffing heavily cuddle up to each other best of friends and then go to sleep. Three weeks later I received a phone call saying that both dogs go out the back of the house and play every day. Still the best of friends!

NEW CHAPTER

There are some people who are concerned about messages that might come through from those who they call bad people. I explain to everyone that I only work with those who are from the light so therefore nobody bad or nasty will come through. Also once the spirit has gone home to the light, (WHICH BY THE WAY IS WHERE EVERYBODY GOES NOWADAYS). They all come with messages from the love & light of all things. Now and again when I explain to one of my clients that a certain person would like to come through with a message if that is okay with them. The client replies "oh, he or she was a very nasty or horrible person when they were alive on the earth plane", or that they had spent a lot of time in jail, or were robbers. I even had one lady say, no way he was a murderer. They all say, why would they want to talk to me anyway. I then explain to them again about whoever and whatever they were on the earth plane, they are now home in the highest realms of love & light. No nastiness, no judgement, no swearing, etc. just love & light. They have been shown who they hurt and loved and also who hurt and loved them. Also they have been shown their whole life from being conceived right up to the time they returned home to heaven, as some people call it. Please remember we are all spiritual beings, having a physical earth experience. Not a physical body having a spiritual experience. (The spirit is continual).

Now going back a few sentences regarding the so called nasty people. Some of these people who lived that type of life, sometimes have messages to pass on to family and friends which are very personal. But also very intelligent, comforting, and also very helpful to the situation that my client is in at that particular time in life. One person I had mentioned a certain name to, was so angry and hateful to that person who had passed over, I had to calm her down and explain that the person in spirit was just trying to say sorry please forgive. My client just replied, "NO WAY, I will never forgive, and also I do not like you for allowing him to even be here". I just replied, "forgiving will set you both free". She said no way and just walked out. Now to let you all know, I have been in that situation before and seen both parties forgive. The transformation that takes place is absolutely amazing. It shows me that is who we all are, a spiritual being of love & light having an earthly experience. Many times I have had a message given to me about someone in this life who was not a very nice person. But in their previous life was just the opposite. Different experiences in different lives are how all souls get to experience all ways of life.

Most people who come to see me accept the messages that they have received and usually say that's them for sure, correct sayings and all. Every now and again I get a client who or whatever, comes through they say "No, not them". Actually they just say no to everything and every message. Even when I see spirit and explain to the client what and who I am seeing them as, the client will agree, but then say no, they wouldn't be here anyway. Most times the spirit coming through will say to me that my client is totally shut off regarding life after the physical, always was. But when the client goes away the thin edge of the wedge is in place. A little bit of wondering got them to come here in the first place. So usually it is just a matter of time, I have had clients return one year later and explain that they didn't believe at first, but lots of strange and interesting times have come up since they saw me last. What it really is, is that their belief system which has been in place since a child, is not quite correct. Much misinformation has been given to them over the years. (Please remember, many years ago the people of the world thought that the land and sea were flat. If you sailed too far out to sea you would fall over the edge!)

This second part of THE MESSAGE BOY II is written by myself, but with all words relayed from my spirit guides, who are from the highest Realms of Love and Light. There are many answers written here to help many of us to understand a little more about who we really are, and why we are here. Some of the stories written here are to explain to all, how many of the world inventions came to be.

Love & Light to all
John Nant.

CHAPTER ONE

A Message From Spirit

ll of us in Heaven would like this book to be written, with love & light and much happiness. Also please listen to your heart regarding this book and all of its messages. Also all of these messages come with truth from what is regarded as the higher realms of what is. Love and light is who all beings are. Many beings regard themselves as more important than others, "NOT SO". Also please remember that all beings have a right. And that is the right to preserve all of

Life. Now as this is a channelled message the words can be spelt in many different ways. In actual fact all of the words have the same meaning. Love and light is who we are, and also love & light is all there is. Some darkness appears periodically, but only as a temporary energy. Many people say to themselves and others that there are equal portions of light and dark. "NOT SO". Far from it. Also many people complain the moment a dark energy of sorts appears in front of them. Also please trust in this as those who do the complaining have not the faith in the love & light of all things. Also the love & light of all things, is just that (ALL THINGS). Also many people who write the same old stories of dark and light being equal is rubbish, in actual fact absolute nonsense.

Now one day a man came to the earth to explain to the people what life was about and also especially why we were here. Within twenty five years of this person explaining to the people, many people agreed. Many of the authorities of the day disbelieved simply because they would be losing their control of all of the people. So therefore he was halted and his physical life on earth was finished. Not only that he was destroyed physically, many of his friends were also. Now this story is well known, many humans also disbelieve in this story, but disbelieving is a part of human nature. The human choice is a gift, As all beings have a survival mechanism built into themselves. Many people will say "rubbish" to these words but the majority already know that is so. Now all people once again have a choice, and that is to help to preserve life or to destroy. Only light will prevail always, and that is so.

And by the way this little story is written by a spiritual guide from the highest of realms. Most people, in fact nearly all people will agree with these words that have been written, and that is a fact of life. Now whether one believes these stories in this book is up to them. Nobody has the right to make them believe or to disbelieve.

One day a very urgent meeting was held in the highest of realms. What this meeting was about is how the earth plane affects all of the rest of the universe. Now then again, many will say what rubbish. But many will agree that there is nobody on this plane who knows, all there is to know. Also there are many messages given to many people by spirit from the light. Most people say thank you and carry on with daily life. Also there are what you would say a handful of people who act upon what they receive. The message here is, it is all the earth people's choice what to achieve by listening or to forget it.

All beings whether physical or inanimate can and have free will. The old stories of control have now finished. The angelic kingdom as I understand has now changed. And as being asked to put this to print, I have agreed. Also many of the old hierarchy have now been moved elsewhere, which means they are still here but with different roles. Many people will disagree, but then again, they are allowed too. Also many people agree because they already know, and that is an actual fact. While this book is being written, thousands of people returned home to the light, and many of those I have spoken to, all say the same. That it is more beautiful here than you could ever dream of. That is to be written for all of those who think, and have been told that they go somewhere else.

As in chapter one, "ALL BEINGS GO HOME". Disbelieved by some means that they think not, but ALAS they do. Many books and teachings say otherwise, but not correct. A certain being who believes that someone else is not fit or good enough to go home to heaven is misleading, and outright selfish. The certain teachings that say that certain people go somewhere else is not correct, "ALL GO HOME". Also many people who have taken their own life for whatever reason is their business and there's alone. Please, everybody has an individual right to do as they please with (their) life. Also please remember, that most people do not like other people telling them what to do, and also those who are reading this book. The readers of this book have the right to read it, throw it away, or to talk about it. 'Please Remember Their Right'. As above, the rights of people, because it is more important as the years go by. As children, they are guided by their peers, and therefore are being taught and shown the ways that their peers know. Also the peer who thinks they know what is right, sometimes do not actually know what is right, but what they have been taught. Also many people think that what they know is correct when actually, it is not so. When one experiences what one has done and also what one has seen, it is actual fact. Which, in other words is the truth to them. Going on with this story relates that many who think that they know only believe that so. And as one knows, to believe is not actually knowing. And also what one would call believing is definitely not knowing. And this is being repeated to let those who say they know and yet have never experienced such, have only a slight idea of knowing. Now then, all of the above is to get people to realise if you have experienced such you then know it. Apart from knowing then you must only Believe. For the simple reason, if you heard about it, read about it, or have been explained to about it, you will then only be able to believe or disbelieve, and that is a fact. The one who remains the knower is also the believer. The other is just the believer. So therefore please allow yourself a little restraint around your knowledge when arguing the point on all matters regarding "Knowing or Believing".

Continuing on fact or fiction, or "I know", or "I believe", please be aware and awake, of how you pronounce your story. As truth is always truth, and untruth can and will cause much distaste in a person who has actually experienced what the conversation is all about. Now automatically the believer will rant and rave for being not knowing. Certain books relate to certain knowing by certain people. Also many books are written by someone's belief of a subject. Many other books are written as Fiction. A story which could be true or not, and most authors have made the story up in their mind. These stories are written up as fiction. An author that has experienced what has actually happened to them is called Fact. The previous book THE MESSAGE BOY, which is, actual and totally fact. Many people have rung and explained how beautiful this book is. Also a few non-believers of spirit have actually enjoyed reading the truth and therefore are looking further into their spiritual self.

Before the first book THE MESSAGE BOY was written many people kept saying that a book should be written explaining the ability to be able to be in touch with the divine essence of love light and healing. Once this book was published, as small as it may be.

People from all over the world have read it with many positive remarks, and this is why a second book has been written due to people asking "When is the next book going to be published?"

Now please listen to the message that has been written. Number 1 Fact or Fiction, Truth or Untruth. Common-sense sometimes does not work for some people. Those people normally live on a belief system not fact.

Once upon a time three angels spoke to me regarding whether or not that I would be interested in helping lost spiritual selves to return home. The answer that I gave was "yes". Also I did ask what it entailed, and then again I felt that it would have been better if I had not asked the last question. Once many things were explained I answered "yes" again. Ever since that day, I felt obliged to listen to what they have to say. Also many beings have talked to me through the guidance of these three guides. The beauty of all of this story is to let people know, that everyone has an Angel with them at all times. An Angel has guidance given to them by the divine himself. Also many people have the ability to talk to their Angel or their guides. Now and again a person who doubts that this story is true appears. Now, over the years the majority of people that I meet, agree. The percentage of disbelievers is around 10%. There are others who totally agree with that 10%, but those people are usually, as paragraph one states, not interested in anything that is truth from someone else. That percentage is around 5%. So overall the majority of people believe in what most humans call the afterlife.

In Australia the Aboriginal people know and have known about those living in the spirit world for many, many years. Many of the Native people in America and Canada also know that there is the spirit world where all Ancestors Reside. And that now brings a short message to the disbelievers. Please trust in the love & light of a creator of pure love & light. Also that when their time here on the earth plane is finishing that they also shall return to the realm of love & light. And that also is for those people who think otherwise. To those people, when they return home to the spirit world usually laugh the most. That is a fact, quoted to me from the Angels that I work with every day, and they are from the most highest of realms. So please do not doubt because there is an afterlife as the Aborigines say, which is so magnificent, you will know when you are home.

Now then, most of this story so far has been published before. But as said again and again more people are believing in life after the earthly plane every day. As such, the more it is realised the higher in vibration the earth becomes and also the people. Now some people say what about the animals? Please believe it or not they already know. Now then, how many people have seen a dog or a cat recognise who they are meeting. Most dogs look at a human about a few feet above the head to see the brightness. If that person receives a very bright light, the dog is automatically friendly. Also please have a look at the amount of wildlife around your house. Now little lizards and others will be proliferent around a well-lit house. Now also the light that shines from an animal or an insect is bright white. Also the fish in the ocean see a different colour to the fresh water fish. The fish in the ocean see an iridescent aqua blue light, and therefore the fish in the freshwater rivers and lakes are seeing white. With all of the animal and insect kingdom, they all understand what these colours mean. Not only the birds and bees but every flower, bush, and tree puts out an aura of love & light. Many people who can see auras will agree to this story. As those who can see, see all of this light whenever they choose too. To look at it, is a slight variation in glancing, that produces the third eye of all beings, to be able to see.

Re a Soul's Journey

Also please listen to what your heart is saying to you regards this spiritual work that you are embarking on. Also the spiritual path that you also are embarking on. Many lifetimes is what the soulself has been doing to retain all of what it knows regarding the creator. The creator is the soulself anyway, so therefore it is experiencing itself physically through each soul. Every soul has a purpose to have itself created anew every time it is reborn as a human being.

The word reborn simplifies the return of the soul to the earth plane. Many people return into the same town as before to finish of a journey which was required to complete over several lifetimes.

History

Many lifetimes ago a certain gentleman arrived as a captain on a sailing ship. He sailed throughout the America's went on then to Australia and also many other parts of the world. This particular soul's journey was to discover many lands that had not previously been occupied apart from the Originals. Many of what you call first settlers were in previous lifetimes the descendants of the originals, and that is how many people feel, and also know that they have been to a certain place on planet earth before.

Once upon a time a little boy whose name we will suppress asked. "What will I be, when I grow up to be a man?" The mother stated, just wait and you will see in fifteen years or so. And with this the little boy said, "I would like to be a carpenter when I grow up. Also I would like to help people with whatever is necessary to make everybody happy". With this the mother replied, "Don't be silly, because you will change your mind lots of times before the time of fifteen years of age". Now the little boy started to cry. "I am going to be a carpenter, he kept saying". "Now stop it!" Replied the mum, "You do not even know what a carpenter is". "I do so", was the reply from the little boy, "because I was one already, because I know". "What do you know?" the mum said. "I was in England and built the great big church that rings a bell every day". With this the mother burst out laughing and replied, "You are too small to even know where England is". "I don't" said the little boy," I just know". The mother scolded the little boy and sent him of to bed. Fifteen years later the same little boy brought home a book from school and stated "There is the building that I built a long time ago". Also the mother repeated the same words and also a similar scolding, and into his room he was sent. Now at the age of twenty one, the boy moved to his auntie's house in England. One day the boy said to his aunty that there was a special gateway tunnel in the church with the big bell that rings every day. With this the aunty who was tuned into the spirit world, just looked at him and said Whereabouts? Nobody knows whereabouts but I know". So off to this building in England the aunty and the boy went. Once they arrived the aunty said, "I know the man who is the caretaker of this particular building." So when all three people met, the little boy who was now twenty one, said to the caretaker about the tunnel. "No my boy, no such thing". So with this the boy showed the caretaker an opening in the back of a special room, moving a painting which had been in the same place for nearly one hundred years. Also this was in fact a painting of the monarch at that time. The entrance was blocked up so no one would ever see it. The boy took away one loose brick. The caretaker told him off for he will lose his job. The twenty one year old said "shine a torch in the space where the brick came from, you will see the steps". So very nervously the caretaker did, and to this very day, the tunnel is now a tourist attraction. The boy is now in spirit and proved to his auntie that he had worked on this building in another lifetime. This building still stands to this day.

Many people will disagree with what is being written in this book. Again and again it shall be written, that all people have a choice, and that is to believe in what is written, or to not believe. Many factions of society will definitely disagree. But more factions do agree. In this book there are many repetitious stories, that is so that many people are to be woken up. Especially to those who have been closed off spiritually through certain ideals.

A New Page a New Story and also a New Way

This is what is happening throughout the universe all of the time. Now once upon a time a certain car named Henry Fords Model A. was just that, a model A. Now Henry Ford knew that he was going to invent the belt of continuous work on a method that no one else had ever tried. This continuous method is now one of the fastest methods of productions for most items. Many of them are cars and many of them are not. But Henry knew the only way to supersede doing or building more than one item at a time was necessary. Now one at a time is okay for a specific model. The family car can now nearly build itself. Also a very, very modern supersonic fighter plane or a jet fighter plane can now be built in fifteen days or less, with the right system in place. Now Henry Ford started all of this method of production. Many of you reading this book will be wondering how this conversation came to be. Well in actual fact Henry Ford had built a method of a conveyer belt in his mind while he was asleep. Guess what! How did spiritually, he become famous? What actually happened, he was downloaded information spiritually, all about how to make a lot of vehicles in a very short amount of time. Most inventions are invented this way. Look at the shape of a stealth bomber, a shape way into the future of modern technology. Also by the way the inventor woke up with this idea of this particular vessel for flight.

Once upon a time in history an inventor explained to the people that the world was round. The people of the day laughed at him, so therefore he kept his information to himself. Several years later a sailor replied to his call, would you be interested in sailing over the edge and having a look at what is there? The sailor replied, "In what?" also, he replied, "what's in it for me?" "Nothing except notoriety and also your own little boat". "Okay" replied the sailor, "I shall have a look". Early in the morning the lone sailor set sail for the edge. During the afternoon a storm came along and blew him out to sea. One month later the sailor returned and to the dismay of all others replied, look what I have found on the shores of another land. A tortoise shell and a large proportion. An evildoer so they called him and then beheaded him. Many years later another gentleman explained to a lone sailor, to sail out from the shores and do not stop. The same scenario, an afternoon storm appeared and out to sea this sailor was blown. Around one year later this particular gentleman sailed his little boat on to the shore of his original departure land. The people were ready to behead this evildoer when a second gentleman who was hiding in the little boat with a third person who happened to be a female, explained to all that were there, where they had come from, there were many more people. Also their lands were available for all to visit. The people on the beach in return, called the three of them from the little boat evildoers and to behead them. Now this story will be repeated further on, different lands, different people, same scenario. The Moral of this story is that it shows how superstition causes everyone to be afraid of anything and anyone that they do not know or understand. In actual fact they all lived in fear. The leader of those people, kept everyone in fear of outsiders so that he could control them all.

Once upon a time a certain person managed to fly, (once again spiritually motivated). This aircraft was designed inside the head of a person, who also agreed that items that were designed in such a way could and should be able to fly like a bird. From then on and through many experiences, one now has the ability to enter space or what some people call outer space. Believe this story or not, it was the start of many, many obligations from life itself, passed through certain people who listened and noted spiritual messages at night while asleep.

TRUE STORY

Once upon a time a lotto was drawn in what we call history. This lotto was, who shall live and who shall not. The dark ages, so it is said, removed thousands of humans through war. These wars are still happening. Many of those whom are reading this book will sit and ponder, what is happening to this spiritual story. Not only pondering but wondering, what is this to do with a message? Just to let all know, as said before, that all life here on the earth and elsewhere is all organised before the actual event. In other words all is written before it happens.

Many lifetimes ago a certain being took a place in the hierarchy of a certain group of people who caused, what is called the death of thousands of people. Many lifetimes after that life the same spiritual journey of that particular soul had one of the most peaceful loveable lifetimes one could ever have. The reason for this type of life was that the one before he had saved thousands of people lives. It is a story to let people know that a soul's journey is that. To experience who it is not and also to experience who it really is, both sides of life, is a fact of life. The most any soul has had in lifetimes on earth and elsewhere is 365. This soul is the most experienced and shall return home to whence it came after this lifetime.

Now most people on the planet earth will agree in these stories of past lives. But many are a little confused on how it all works. This book is to help many of those people who already know how it works to the best of their knowledge. Also to those who would like to know. Love and Light, and that is all there is.

Now many will disagree. If one chooses to be what some say, gone to the dark side, in actual fact it is just a part of a creator who is pure love & light. Once again the Creator of all is pure LOVE & LIGHT. Rest assured that this is so. Also the universe is made up of all energies. Negativity is a minor part of life. Not even. Not a major part, it is a by-product of what people call evil. Most people are in their thinking, love & light. Certain beings are experiencing the opposite, but still are the derivative of love & light, and are love & light. Now and again there is a period in time where darkness, or what one would call a negative time is greater than normal. But still is not and never will be greater than the love & light of all things. Once upon a time, a certain being created a war of massive proportions. All the people apart from his people blamed him for all of the misery. Now on a spiritual level, everyone had agreed to experience who they are not, and that believe it or not, is how life is.

Once upon a time a very musical gentleman wore a piano necklace around his wrist. What this means is that he played a piano all day and half of the night. During his life he noted several notes and tunes that no one had ever dreamed about. Most of the music is still to this day, the most complicated music to play. Once he played his piano in front of Kings and Queens, and also to nearly every royalty in the world. This music was downloaded spiritually during the night to his physical spiritual self, by guides of his from the highest of realms. Same scenario, a fact of life.

Once upon a time a certain lady,

whose name shall be kept out of this book, arrived at a meeting in America. This lady happened to be from America. Her friend by the way was English. Many years before this particular day, the English lady had a vision of being in America. The two women had met in a shop on a cruise ship sailing around the world. The first time that they met, it was just a polite "Hello my name is ----- ------ and you are Mary from England". With this Mary looked at the American lady and replied, "your name is also the same as mine". They both laughed and replied to each other at the same identical time. I feel you and I are sisters. Now with this story it lets people know that there is no such item which people call a coincidence. Everything on the earth plane is organised on a spiritual level before one even arrives. Once upon a time most humans knew this and also since the days of more understanding and being allowed to. More people agree every day.

Many, many years ago there was a land named ATLANTIS. The days were long and also were very warm. The Crystal Kingdom of Atlantis is actually a true and faithfully, exactly correct place. The word faithfully comes from this message which the majority of readers realise, that these stories are being relayed from a higher source of love & light. Once upon a time the world was in a part of a solar system which has changed over the centuries. The scientists of today have arrived at a conclusion which in actual fact is not quite correct. It is close but a long way off what is being said. There was a gentleman named Newton who in actual fact was a past life being from Atlantis. Many people will agree and others shall not. This particular gentleman was fed the information from his spiritual self at night time. Long ago this was given to many others, and like today most cannot be bothered, or else too concerned what others will say, and also how the authorities would handle such information. A million years ago was Atlantis's sister state which also disappeared. The reason of the disappearance of both was an explosion.

Not as thought by others to still be here on planet earth.

Once upon a time several galaxies were involved in a mass execution of time all at once, which means an explosion took place and altered the whole universe. Many people today call it the big bang. Also many people disbelieve in that theory. Those who thought or think that is not correct are in fact not correct themselves. Many scientists believe that this so called big bang was in actual fact the beginning of mankind, but also not correct. Mankind began a lot earlier than that. A different type of man which some people would call not human, but they also would be and are not correct. Since the beginning of time, which by the way is the beginning of all things, is in actual fact just the beginning of time and nothing else. Beings have been living on other planets for millions and millions of years. Many years ago the first bang was just the beginning of a being with two legs and two arms. The second big bang changed the shape of many beings. Many beings including humans have been living for millions of years. The first human described as just a monument of what a human actually was. Not the story of two humans suffering under a rule, that story of the blame for everyone else is absolutely not correct. How could only two beings be the cause of billions of people? (please think about it). A long time ago a certain being tried to explain but to no avail. Certain groups detested the sight and the right of another human's ideas. Now this particular person was in fact a very advanced soul, with a journey to try to teach humanity about life itself. And today there are many people trying very hard to do the same. Another person well before the last one mentioned also did the same. This person lasted four weeks walking a desert, and then received a message from spirit, that what he was trying to achieve, was in actual fact a waste of time. On returning with information on life itself he was then laid to rest by the authorities. In present time which happens to be now and at this point in history, a person advanced as spiritually as both of the two beings mentioned, would be able to express their views freely in two thirds of the world. Now the other one third is not advanced as spiritually as the others. Also they have in those countries a certain system in place so that no one can even speak about life itself.

Now once upon a time a spiritual mentor was just that. Many native civilisations always had a Medicine man or a Shaman, man or woman which helped them with their spiritual life. Along time ago one of the native shaman of a well-known tribe, explained to the people about the modern civilization that was appearing in his subconscious mind. Four hundred years later all came to fruition that was forecast. His spiritual self was explaining to the physical spiritual self the story of the future.

One night a holy man explained to the people that the weather was going to be dreadful, Windy, raining. One of the townspeople replied. "What you mean is that the weather will be wild, wet and windy". "No," was the reply, "dreadful". A third person stood up and replied. "No such item, all weather is beautiful, the sun and the water is required to help our food supply grow. The wind is there also to clean our crops of insects". With this the holy man replied, "No way, it is the wrath arriving, for everyone has not been as true to life as they should." A fourth person stood his ground and replied, "Rubbish you talk as if everyone here is bad". The holy man replied "That is so, so please sit down". And with this the whole town stood up and walked away. Now the moral of this story is that one person's ideas are not necessary correct, compared to everyone else's ideas. There is no such item as correctness by everyone and all will agree with this statement unless you don't. That is a fact.

Many lifetimes ago a certain human being walked around certain parts of the planet looking for enlightenment. After several years, he sat down under a tree and with this he burst out laughing. He laughed and then cried and then laughed for many days. Once most of the tears had subsided, he burst out laughing. For the simple reason is, what he was looking for, he himself already knew. Now this story is to let people know that if you understand that all items in life are spiritual. You are already enlightened. And that is what he was laughing about. Now for many days this particular spiritually in-tune person relayed messages from the spirit world to others, which is now known as a script. And that is all due to one being in tune totally with life itself. Now another once upon a time story, the gentleman who sat under the tree is very revered all around the world. Now most people would not understand what this story is all about, but the gentleman himself had seven more lifetimes after that episode of walking the land and then sitting under a tree. This particular day in 2017 this gentleman is an Angel of the highest order.

Many years ago a certain lady created a name for herself as helping many, many wounded soldiers. Her name is also very well known, and just to let the majority of people know, this particular Angel of a lady is now living in the highest realm of love & light. This also is after three more lifetimes, from that particular time of helping many other humans.

Once upon a time a certain lady was naming a particular son of hers, a very feminine name. This particular son, abused his mother when he got old enough to realise what the name meant. The real issue was to do with humiliation, and that is what the soul's journey was requiring at that particular time in life. Also his sister who had a very masculine name requiring her to change her name to another. With this the mother was very angry, also so was the father. The daughter rebelled and went on in history to conquer many lands for the sake of her beloved country. The soul's journey was satisfied with the outcome for the simple reason was the journey in itself.

On a lighter note these stories are true also as it happened. Many of you will ask yourselves who in history are these people in this book. The reason there are no names is that the spiritual soul who past forward this information does not choose to deliberate the names of all concerned. Many of these stories, one can look up on a computer if they choose to. No names are to be given to any pages and that is how one will find out for themselves. By asking their own guides and that is if their guides choose to deliberate this information. The moral of this story is to get most people thinking. Not that many people require this exercise, but to try to reach out to people who are reading this book, to try and receive messages from spirit themselves. And that is all on the message department.

Once upon a time a certain gentleman of much wealth created a machine, which to this day has never ever been released. This machine is very similar to a computer. The modern computer is very much the same type of machine, in actual fact very, very much like it. Once a computer creates another computer the world will never ever be the same again. Now modern technology is just that, modern. Old machines are just that, old machines. Now the moral of this story is such that the first gentleman who made a certain machine is now very, very happy, for the simple reason his original ideas on communication has finally been realised. The inventor in the late 15th century was in actual fact a believer that all things were possible. Just look at what has happened in the communication field today. The modern computer is in actual fact the most intricate piece of machinery; already it has superseded expectation from the original builder. Now please by the way explain to yourself how a computer works, and then allow yourself a lot of time to imagine how somebody would come up with the knowledge of how to build such an item.

Also another machine was placed in a library beside many books, and to this day has never ever been seen. The books were in a private library disguised as a laundry cupboard in Pennsylvania. This machine would change the shape of telescopes. The reason for this story is that the spirit self would like this discovery to be made.

Now and again a certain discovery gets put away, for the inventor feels that he is far too way out, or else he feels that the people are not quite ready. On a regular basis a discovery is found to be of no avail or of use to mankind in present time.

Once upon a time this particular inventor invented the light bulb. Now to this day everyone uses this method of lighting. Into the future I shall write a story regarding the new light bulbs, which hardly look like the bulbs used today, and also hardly use electricity at all. Many people have tried to reclaim the use of a light bulb in many different ways, the closest to the new way of the bulb in the future is the L.E.D lighting system. Once these systems are in place, no power is required. An itinerary of the system will be produced in the very near future.

Once also was a gentleman and his wife who on a regular basis drove one of the first motor cars in Europe to a place of intrigue. This place holds many secrets in many hidden compartments. These hidden compartments will also be found in the very near future. Also the gentleman, who wrote this story in spirit, would love people to find time for themselves to think about the stories in this book. Many people have many brilliant ideas to help mankind, and due to many factures, feel unreliably very careful to indulge their secrets.

The majority of ideas are squashed and therefore in spirit, are sitting in the atmosphere waiting to be produced at another time. Please remember all of these stories are being relayed by the spirit world for those who are interested in what is regarding Life Itself.

Not too long ago a gentleman asked to see the world. His mother said, "Why Son, what is it that you would like to see?" "The whole world" was his reply. "Why?" His mum replied, "Don't we have everything here that is required for having a great time? Not only that, we have money, sunshine, surf, fishing, mountain climbing, and many other items of interest". "Well," said the gentleman, "a man has to achieve what one feels like achieving, otherwise when I am old I may regret not doing what I would have liked to". "Well," said the mother, "off you go and here is some money. Please, please enjoy and I shall think of you always". The moral of this story is to please, please let people be aware of another's journey. The lady in the story was the mother with great respect for another human's life path. Even as though it hurt her very much to lose her son.

Many lifetimes ago and into the 1700's a gentleman and his wife rode a certain type of bicycle. This bicycle reminded both of them what they had both seen in a dream. Both people remembered how to make this bicycle in the morning of the dream. They drew a picture of what they had both seen that night on the ground, and then they both laughed. "What is it?" the lady replied. "I don't know said the" gentleman and so they discarded all of what they drew. A year later same again, except this time they drew it on paper. A moment after they had finished, a neighbour who had come to visit replied. I think it is a new type of bicycle. With this they all laughed and then went back to a shed to start building their new bike. The reason for this story is all of the plans of this particular bike came in a dream state given to them by spirit at night time.

Now then, once upon a time a story was told of a little boy with a cow. This little boy happened to trade his cow for some so called magic beans. After his mother had told him off he decided to climb the beanstalk. Now this story relates to most people today. Most people organise themselves and then rearrange all of their ideas and change what we call your mind. After changing your minds, most people say many times, "I should have carried on with my first plan, what a mess I am in now", and therefore have created a situation just like the little boy with the cow on his way to the market. He swapped, and look what happened to him. Everybody who has read this story of Jack and the Beanstalk realises how silly that he was. Now then the moral of this story is. Usually your first choice or first decision to do what it is that you are trying to achieve is the correct one. Simply your spiritual self has explained on another level which way to go. After that the conscious mind rules and after that nothing. So therefore your first choice is and usually is the correct choice. The conscious mind can and will change at whim.

The next story relates to how life treats people according to others. Many people will say, "How lucky they are they just won a lottery, look at us we buy twice as many tickets as they do, so why them?" Well in actual fact the divine essence itself has guided those people to buy a ticket in a certain lottery, at a certain time, from a certain shop. NOW PLEASE TRUST. Everybody has guidance, and therefore on a spiritual level are meant to receive everything that they actually receive. NO MORE, NO LESS.

Starting a new paragraph regarding the weather. Now most people at some time in their life have complained about the weather many times. Too hot, Too cold, Too wet, Too windy, or else just hopelessly wrong with the weather forecast. And many people just complain about all of it. The weather itself, believe it or not is actually live spiritual energy.

Now some of you will say rubbish its water from the rain and when the sun's out, that's how it is. "WRONG". The plane of this planet controls all of it. If there is a drought which people are suffering then that is so. Also vice versa. If it rains so much, the flooding hurts many people. Now and again a wind will arrive in such a way it shall blow many buildings over. With this wind, everyone complains because all the buildings have been demolished. If one person becomes ill or happens to finish their life on this plane because of the wind, this particular wind is called deadly. Now after every gigantic storm right throughout the world, there is much work. Now and again a different view of life is also gathered amongst all the people involved. Many states in America that have tornadoes are then re-examined and then built again, to the amazement of others in the world. They get rebuilt, redesigned, restrengthened, but mostly to how the people perceive their life to be, and therefore build in the same place as before. Many storms throughout the world have destructively demolished buildings, just to be rebuilt on the same land as before. But usually with a different attitude with the people, and also a different outlook towards life. And as one knows, one could be here today and finished on the earth plane tonight. Now the moral of this story is, please remember that all living beings can and will always regard life firstly above all things. Just to reiterate this story all of the people of America see many storms every year. Not one person stops living because a storm is coming, they just do whatever is necessary to survive.

Once upon a time a certain Angel approached a certain lady regarding a way and a method of approaching an army that was ready to attack and destroy a certain civilisation. This particular lady was ready to listen, and so with great intrigue a certain strategy was put in place, and the approaching army laughed. Within one week the approaching army was decimated and the lady was the country's hero. Now please read this carefully. One Angel's advice rectified a karmic debt owed from one country to another and, believe this or not, as rectified totally. And therefore one country in the future ended up being a very friendly neighbour, and to this day still is. Now everyone who has read this will realise who this particular lady was, and also those who have decided to believe this to be true (which by the way is) are now opened to realise that debts get repaid, whether it is now or in the future. Many people believe it all happens in the lifetime that they are in." But Not So ". Love & Light.

Many years ago a certain general

survived a horrific battle, and also many other skirmishes. Once the general retired and went home to his family, a neighbour accidently shot him dead and also his wife. What had happened to them, happened karmically from what the general had done during the lead up to the war. This particular general raided a property that he liked and then stole the land claiming it was his. Once the war broke out he then received the ownership papers to the land falsely, and this story is by the way absolutely truthful. And also as others know, it is to let you know that what you do to others you do to yourselves.

Once upon a time a certain lady rode a horse totally naked through the city streets. After being dismounted from the horse, a certain gentleman offered to loan her an overcoat. Once the overcoat was in place, the officials at that time came to arrest her. With this the gentleman whom offered her the coat laughed profusely and then took his own coat and wrapped it around the lady. This particular gesture was applauded by all of those who were watching. The establishment was in actual fact three other gentlemen. When they seized the lady, all of the people watching gathered in close and told the three law men not to touch her. With this the whole town received a notice of infringement. Now to finish this story is to show the ridiculous encounters of three was thwarted by a whole town of people. (who is correct?) Well the law stated, no nudity was allowed, but also that law happened to be made by a lady of the establishment only. On request that lady was asked to stand down, when she replied "No", the townspeople then threw her out, not the lady on the horse. Now the moral of this story is the majority so they say, have the say. In present time the majority are the ones who select the very small few to make the rules. These small few always seem to think that they can overrule the majority. Tough Luck, that attitude does not work in modern society and that is all. That particular story was put in this book to let a certain amount of people, whom think that they know everything that there is to know, and also those same people to realise that they are only people. Same as everyone else, nothing more and also nothing less. If this paragraph annoys you, would you please, please realise that it is no joke. And please wake up to yourselves. And that is all.

Once upon a time a certain lady controlled most of a country. Several others were helping until one of the others decided 'her' idea of running a country was far more aggressive, but far more progressive. Another lady disputed the second lady but got caught and was executed by the second lady. Another lady in the group found out what happened and then explained to the ruler of the country what was happening. Now with this the ruler thanked the informer, executed the second lady and all of her followers. Now one and a half years later a war broke out and in that country that is being written about. Anarchy started to rise. The first lady or ruler was then creating an army to dispel all of the aggression which was created by the execution of one man. The world knows of this story and therefore many people started to realise, that the women of the world were as important and as strong as their male counterparts. The Moral of this story, is please and I say please respect both sexes. Eventually the lady who was the leader conquered all opposition and also a fellow country, with whom the people were planning to take over." History It Is Written". All of this story is 100% True. Please remember the right type of person always ends in power one way or another, and also please remember in most countries the people decide who this particular person may be. Also without upsetting many other people, it is about time that dictator leaders get shown that the people are the ones whom let them stay in power.

Once upon a time a certain gentleman called to the stars to guide him safely on his journey through the night. Around midnight a falling star shot through the sky, the gentleman took this as a sign from heaven. He altered course with his yacht or (sailing boat) to a direction of the falling star. When morning arrived he was very close to a land that had never been registered on any chart. With this he started to draw a new chart, and working with the sun of the angle of its arising drew an island. Four days later, after sailing around a certain island he called it HAWA'II. And then again, he called on the stars to guide him further afield. Within a three month period a certain gentleman had discovered the Hawaiian Islands. Spiritually he had received messages from spirit all the way throughout his journey. IT IS CALLED TRUST IN LIFE.

Once upon a time many sailors roamed or sailed all around the world.

As all knows the planet earth is mainly water. Two thirds of the water is salted. Many items of discovery still remain hidden under the ocean. Many years from now a certain gentleman shall come across many, many treasures. One gentleman spent many years investigating many of Earth's waters. This gentleman was a Frenchman of the highest order, a gentleman and also a very good mariner. Many times the gentleman made production movies and videos of the undersea life of the planet earth. He and his sons roamed, sailed, and motored on many oceans, much of his discoveries have been shown on TV. The many discoveries that he and other divers have with them, are memories. Those memories still go out into the universe and therefore belong to that human. When one goes home, and that is to the realm of pure love & light, all of the thoughts and memories nowadays goes with them. Lifetimes ago those thoughts and memories stayed in the planet Earth's atmosphere. A little like what people describe as a cloud a computer sets up. A cloud of knowledge and people can access that information from that cloud. Now all of a sudden many of you reading this book will realise that what you put out verbally or mentally you own. A Hard Thought, for some. Now those whom are destined to be abused through life, can access this cloud and make amends spiritually and karmically. Also many recommendations from certain authorities will also agree. Now also there shall be some resistance by certain factions. Those who object will also now realise that their objections belong to them, and therefore it would be up to them to remove certain thoughts which are not correct. When one says out loud or quietly to themselves, I was wrong with certain thoughts, the original thoughts get cancelled. A long period of time to come of corrections. Therefore please and I will say please consider carefully your words and thoughts.

Once upon a time a certain gentleman regarded all of his possessions as his own. His wife used to say to him, why do you always regard everything that we own as yours? The gentleman replied, well you stayed at home and cleaned the house and I went to work, so therefore everything that I do re earning finances is mine. With this the lady packed her bags and left. After three months this lady met a man who was very opposite in his way of thinking to her ex-husband. The lady explained to her new friend about the way her husband thought. Now the gentleman was laughing so much he forgot to say, that he used to be like that until his wife left. The moral of this story is to let most readers and others to understand. If you feel like everything is yours you will lose all of it. Also, if you lose your wife's share as well, you only lose half of what you have achieved in obtaining. 'NOW' please read again and work out the moral of this story.

Once upon a time an Irishman got zapped with electricity by an orthopaedic surgeon. The reason being named like this, was that the man in question who did the zapping, at what many people call a mental facility, some even call it a mental asylum, and many other words describing a place where so called mentally ill people can go to. Now to get to the point, this Irishman had a problem mentally, so the so called experts had diagnosed personally. All he did was to be against all of his friends' thoughts and ideas regarding his family

and also his so called responsibilities.
The Irishman felt by himself the right
for him to hop in a car and to drive to a
destination that he always wished that he
could go to. And then when he did, his
so called friends told the authorities that
he had lost the plot and was travelling
recklessly all around a certain country.
When certain authorities caught up
with the Irishman, they took him to a
mental disabilities establishment. Then
started to proceed with giving electric
shock treatment (so they call it) to the
Irishman to try to get him to understand
that you do not just drive your car willy
nilly around your country. Now after
many so called shock treatments, the
Irishman just let go of his will to live and

then passed over into a different realm. Now the moral of this story which is 100% true, is to let the establishment know spiritually who gave them the right to do such atrocities to someone who was having family problems and felt like getting away. He had his own money, own car, and paid for everywhere he went, and then after a while when he did return all of his friends belittled him. On a spiritual level the Irishman was trying to achieve a dream. He achieved his dream and then was betrayed.

Once upon a time stories are just that. True stories but once upon a time. The years and the dates are irrelevant due to the time and space of all things. Please remember that time is just that, Time.

Also Space is just Space and according to all things there is no such item as space. People realise that if standing in one particular space or a particular part of space and then move, they are standing in a different part of what you call space. In that part that you call space are millions upon millions of particles. So really there is no space. Hypothetically space is that where there is nothing, and in reality there is no such place as space. Space itself does not exist.

Once upon a time a certain well known bandit (so the people called him), also another you would call a very indecisive male worked together to terrorize the people. After many years of robbery and rape the two males got caught. As they were hanging, a certain judge claimed that the jury was paid off. Now with this the people got a knife and cut down the two so called bandits. Now the reason that the judge called out, was that his brother was on the jury, and with a guilty conscience he let his brother the judge know that the mayor of the town paid a certain amount of money to be divided with the jury. Once it was discussed and also placed in the local newspaper of the day, the mayor was hung. Now the moral of this story is two bandits nearly hung by the townspeople were then released. From that moment on the two bandits stopped robbing and raping and turned themselves into what people say decent citizens. Now that moral is the story all beings can change. The certain circumstances came about by townspeople forgiving, except the mayor. This particular mayor was voted by the crooks that ran the businesses in the town. Not only that, the two bandits only robbed the business people. Now to finish off this story, who was in the wrong, the thieves of business men or the bandits? This story is about forgiveness and finding out the truth. We are Love and Light.

This book is continuing to be written at a time of many distractions. A certain lady of wealth shall create a moment for others to realise that all work that is being done, is to help others realise who everyone really is, and that is spiritually.

Many years ago this project was started in America, and now many people from all over the world are starting to realise that all beings can be spoken to, all animals also. Once upon a time far back in history many of the Aboriginal tribes throughout the world used to do this every day. Nowadays the process is returning and also to be written for all beings to realise this part of life. A certain being of wealth as written earlier will help many people on their way. Love and Light is who we all are despite what is happening at present time throughout the world.

Once upon a time and also into the future, many people will be ostracised by certain factions of the public, who in actual fact have no idea who they really are. And as on many occasions, those who know the least speak the loudest. As indicated by many nowadays whom are realising that there is life after the physical, and also regards to a spiritual realm, can actually now speak out about their spiritual experiences without being ridiculed or persecuted. The time in history is here for all beings to raise their consciousness to a much higher level than ever before. Many people will disagree but then again as human beings have done for many years, put their head in the sand so to speak regarding anything to do with the spirit world. Also anything to do with what is not written. Now please remember this story is not written to abuse what already has been written, but it is now written to let people realise that much that has been written in the past is not so. Love and Light please remember, this is who we all are.

Now once again please remember that this book has been written to explain to the many who earth beings really are. A spirit does not ever cease to exist, a physical can last up to a maximum of over one hundred years, but not too many over one hundred. Please remember that others that have had many experiences with the spirit world, also have been given the same information. This lady whom it has been written about previously in this chapter, organises many others out of their fear of what people call death, and into a realisation that exists continually for millions of years. That in itself is a very valuable contribution to life itself. End of this chapter and now the new chapter is to help others to be able to realise that all can talk to all. This story will relate to experiences from the author.

TALKING TO ANIMALS

A few months ago a lady rang me and asked if I could tune into one of her dogs. She had four of them, but one was limping badly and also was looking a little bent. I tuned into the dog that was limping and it explained to me, that the biggest dog jumped of the lounge seat and landed on top of her. Also she has a broken leg. I repeated this information to the lady and she replied, "I have caught the big dog doing that before with the other dogs. The big dog has its favourite chair and won't let any of the other dogs near it". I then said to the lady, "I am getting that you can talk to your dogs spiritually and that they talk back to you, is this correct?" "Yes," she replied "but I never thought of asking as I am in a bit of stress around my little dog." "Well," I said "how about asking the little dog is what you just heard correct." "I already have while you were talking and the little dog replied 'yes, he is a big bully'." "Well please go and ask the big dog, did he yes or no?" The lady went into the lounge and started laughing. She said, "You should be here John, the big dog knows that I know and its head is down on its feet looking as guilty as." I then heard the lady telling the big dog off and to stop picking on the others. The lady then back on the phone again said, "I asked the big dog and he said yes but was only playing and didn't mean to hurt it." So with this the lady off to the vet to get the broken leg and dislocated back attended to. Two months later the lady rang me to tell me all was well again and all dogs were happy. It just cost around three and a half thousand dollars.

A lady rang me a few months ago regarding a little problem with one of her race horses. I went around to the lady's house and at the back of the property were eleven stables. As I walked past all of the horses they all looked at me as if they all wanted to talk to me. When we got to the particular horse regarding the so called problem, the lady then said "it is a very good race horse but will not run any good in the rain. Why? Could you please try to find out why." So with this I looked at the racehorse and asked if I could come into the stable with it and all being peaceful. "Yes" was the reply," come in no trouble." The lady said, "not many people can go into her stable as she does not like it." I opened the gate, went in and put my hand on her head, then I put the other hand on top of her left leg. "What's up with not wanting to run in the rain I asked?" "I don't like the rain and it started when I was little and nearly drowned." "Ok," I replied, "anything else you would like to say?" "One more bucket of water per day and another half bucket of food. Love racing,

Love the owner and that's all." So with this I did a healing on the horse then walked out of the stable, shut the gate and just looked at the horse. It came straight up to the gate put its head on my shoulder and cuddled into the side of my head. "All will be well and next time in the rain I will be fine thank you." After explaining all the messages to the lady, she said "I will ring up the people that I bought her off and ask what happened when the horse was little." Both of us went into her house for coffee and the lady rang the previous owner. After lots of sighs and laughter over the phone the lady came back into the dining room and said. "Well I'll be darned, when that horse was little it happened to rain for many days and the farm was totally flooded. The horses had to swim to an island which really was a small hill on the property and also many other animals had the same idea. Lucky the rain stopped or else some of them could have drowned." I then explained if one tune's into the universe a little more, one could speak to all of her horses. I spoke to the lady a few weeks later and she said that the horse got a third placing in the wet.

Messages From Guides

Once upon a time a person who spoke to others about what has been written in this book would have been persecuted and mostly executed. This now will allow many factors to be written which were never allowed to be written before. Now what this means is that realising that this book can now be written without persecution is to show how much more advanced the people have come regarding spirituality. Many factions also will disagree to any part of this book simply because they still believe in what was written earlier in time. Also now this is okay, but please remember what was written then, was not exactly as it was. It was written by man with the limited knowledge of what was handed down through the ages. And now if one is wondering why all of this information is now coming to be written, please remember in history, if one wrote about spirituality one was not here for very long. Also man has changed his way of thinking simply because he is allowed to.

Another once upon a time story. A little man with a very big heart stopped a nation from receiving many bad depts. The politicians of the day were very corrupt and also they were very rich. Another gentleman explained to the little man what was happening to all the land and the poverty of the people. The little man rode on his horse to have a look at the poverty and the way the authorities were handling them, 'them' being the people. As he rode, a young lady came up to him riding on another horse. "What do you think about all of the peasants?" she said. He replied to this lady, "What are peasants?" With this the lady burst out laughing and said, "You must be one of them." The little man said to the lady "Are you one too?" And with this the lady rode away. Now then the little man went to the next town and bought all of the farm land around the town. Several days later the little man came across the lady previously on the horse. "Hello" he cried. "Get lost" she replied, "peasant". So to stop the story which is very true. The gentleman that he was, explained to the lady, "Please hop off your horse and say sorry." Now with this her brother who had arrived in the meantime said to the little man, and then argued about why speak to his sister that way. "Are you a peasant?" said the little man. "No, I am not," was the reply from the brother, "I am the owner of all of that land over to the right". "Well," said the little man "I am the owner of all that you can see on the left of you, plus in front of you, and also from behind you". Now with this the lady apologised and then tried to woo the little man into a relationship. The little man looked at the lady and replied. "BUZZ OFF PEASANT!" And that concludes this story. Now the moral of this story is to let everyone know that everyone is a peasant some time in life simply for spiritually, you are all equal.

Now to those who are finding this book plus this story okay to read. It will leave you with a little knowledge, re who everybody is. Now to those who do find it disturbing or not very interesting, or actually think that most stories are incorrect, will realise at a later date you have been hoodwinked into believe that yourself is not spiritually inclined. But also not quite ready in life to realise who you really are. LOVE & LIGHT

Going back a few pages I explained that all beings are Love and Light. Now many people shall have a different opinion to that saying. Please remember that this book is related to who everyone and everything is spiritual. If all was perfect on the earth plane, there would be nothing to experience by coming to this plane. All is well, in all realms to the maker's design. So please remember, all is to experience who you are not really, but also to experience Love and Light in the physical.

When will life realise that life is all that there is. Life realises itself for the simple reason it is what it is. Many people say that life is too hard, others reply to that saying, life is magnificent, others do not seem to worry about life, it exists for all to enjoy. Now while all are reading this paragraph, which person are you? One, Two or Three? Then again you may be all. What this is about is to realise that life is just life all concepts. Hot or Cold, Large or Small, also Good and Very good, because to life itself there is no bad. Only beings with a certain consciousness will say that something or someone is bad. In actual fact there is no such item of consciousness in life's view as bad. Sounds strange but that is so. Love and Light is who we all are and Love and Light is what life is.

Once upon a time a certain gentleman

claimed all of Europe could be unified as one country. Many years later another gentleman claimed the same, but forgot to ask all of the different types of people who lived there. Now this story is not a joke, true to be exposed in history. The first gentleman passed over not very long after the announcement. The second gentleman did the same. Throughout history there has always been somebody with a certain idea of unification, and now there is a movement of the same, throughout Europe. But a referendum for the very first time was requested, and the answer to that question re the whole of Europe being as one was rejected. What this actually means is, for the very first time in history the people of a country were asked. Now why this story has been so to speak brought to the light, is that history is now being made by certain authorities asking the mass population for their ideas on the life that they would like to be a part of. Also for the very first time it was shown that many of the people are divided in there way of thinking. Again history was made by a certain politician for the very first time again, to ask the people in general their ideas altogether. The answers were left to the mass population. One part said yes, another replied no, and another did not even bother to answer. Now again why this story? It is to let people know how history changes through time. What in fact is fanatical this year, can be the opposite next year. Life itself does this to let all know that life itself, Never and repeat Never stands still. It is called reproduction. Now Here, Gone tomorrow. New day, New Year, New Hour, and new ideas, and also New Ideals.

Many lifetimes ago a certain gentleman arose and conquered all of his opposition. The opposition at that time were the religious factions. Most of these being a certain type of religion, wanted this gentleman put away. The outcome of this situation was this certain person, which some called a gentleman named the king, was the king. This particular king got married several times, the religions of the day back-pedalled many steps until he spoke one day and replied to them all. "It is my life not yours, and as you know, I am the King and you are not." With all the factions of religion he split. "What we will do," he said, "It shall be known as My Way, or another way of putting it, AS I SAY OR ELSE." What happened was or "else" mainly, and a little of my way. The factions remained united for a while, and went their own way. After a while this king vanished from sight due to illness, when these factions heard of this, they then fought each other thinking that they could run the country. But and then they forgot that the king was still the king. In actual fact it was a ploy by the king to see if he could trust any of the factions. But alas, no was the outcome, so the majority were expelled from life. Now then again, who is right? The factions with their ideals or the king. This particular king said to all. "I am the king so therefore all ideals are to be shown to me", and with this he passed a law. All people interested in changing my ideals will be listened to and then put to death. He then laughed and smiled and went on governing his country in a very productive manner. The moral of this story is, who gives the authority to allow another so called authority the right to declare that a certain king should listen to them.

Once upon a time story again. This one relates to a certain lady who conquered her neighbours by allowing many people to walk through her property to a certain seaside holiday beach. Now to reach the outcome of what this story is about is to relay the truth. A particular neighbour asked this particular lady if she would sell her farm to him. "No," was her reply. "You will close the access road to the people's holiday beach." The answer to her was, that is correct, we as a family want the beach for ourselves. "Well," said the lady, "no deal, in actual fact I myself will loan the council some money to buy from me the access road." The angry neighbour replied, "Great, I am standing for the council member for this area, the moment I am elected I shall get the road closed." "Now then replied the lady, I shall not sell at all so BUZZ OFF!" The angry neighbour went to the council and offered a portion of his land for an access road to the beach with mind to make some money, and to annoy his elderly lady neighbour. This he did, and also a little shack that he himself owned and built on the beach. When the real estate started to market the angry neighbour's property, the lady went and bought all that was for sale. 'Unknown' was written on the contract of the land. After a while the new owner who was the lady, donated the roadway and the shack on the beach to her family. A month later her so called angry neighbour called out to the lady, "what are your family members doing on that land? I have sold it." "I know," the lady replied, "My son and daughter bought it." With this the angry neighbour sold all of his property and then moved elsewhere. After a few months, the elderly lady passed to another realm and donated her part of the land to the council as a park and a holiday beachside camp ground. Now the moral of this story is to let everyone know, that there is always a peaceful way around all areas of life. Love & Light

Another once upon a time story. Many people realised that the ocean was a means of travel. The very first sailing ship carried fifteen people from one land to another. This very first occasion an ambassador arrived by sailing boat on the shores near a European city. In this city lived many superstitious, very religious beings. After meeting the sailors the townspeople slaughtered them all. Apparently according to the leader of the people the sailors were all heathens, and not only that, they were evil doers from another time. After many years another sailing boat sailed to the same destination. On arriving many spears and arrows were directed at the sailors. With this, the sailors turned around and sailed back to where they came from. The excitement of the people on the land when they returned, was simply because the sailors had returned home safely. The captain of this particular sailing vessel also happened to be a leading warrior. After he had visited his master, as he called him, they came to the conclusion that all their other sailing boats and family who sailed, were massacred by the people over the other side of the sea. Now same as before in a previous story. All the captain was required to do, he did, and that was to build fifteen more sailing vessels twice as big, and then filled every sailing vessel with food, water, swords, spears, and also many trained soldiers. After one whole year all were completed. With this exercise being completed they all sailed to the same land as before. Only one difference, when they all arrived a mercenary arrived to the sailors in a very small boat and asked if they could take him on board. "Well," replied the captain, "who are you and why do you ask?" "Well," replied the mercenary, "many people are on the shore waiting to throw spears and arrows at you all, and I myself rowed out here to you to escape. For the simple reason myself and twenty five others sailed here last week, and I have actually been rowing since then." After he explained to the captain about the type of people who lived on the shores and how fanatically religious they were, yet they killed all of the other sailors. Now, this captain, as explained before, was also a warrior. The captain then got a message to all of his ships to now fight to the end or turn around. The message received from the other captains was to fight, for the simple reason many of their friends did not return home from other sailing excursions. So with this, all the sailing vessels anchored outside of a bay and two hundred soldiers went ashore. As the arrows started to fly, the sailors let go many arrows also, and a battle raged for three days. The captain of the expedition put up a white flag for truce. What happened then is also a memory for history. As the people on the beach tore down the barricade and rushed with swords flashing at the flagbearer thinking that was the end of the trouble makers, two hundred of the people from the beach ran towards fifteen sailors. As they arrived close enough to see what was happening it was too late. The sailors who were fighting them, arrived from behind the forest and wiped out every religious fighter, and then proceeded into the town and also wiped out every male. The main captain went straight to where the leader of the shore people was and asked. "Why do you attack boats, when you do not know, what or who is inside them?" "They are all evil," replied the town leader, "all of them, because if they were not evil I would have been told." "By whom?" replied the captain, "By the almighty himself" was the reply from the town leader. "Well," replied the captain, "the almighty is with us today for the simple reason, we have been praying for many days for this moment. So therefore you lose and goodbye to your head." With this a new country was founded by sailors for the very first time. Now also the moral of this story is to please find out the real truth before one sets out to destroy. And this story is the truth, and also written in certain history books.

Many years ago a certain gentleman wrote a book regarding Guardian Angels. All human beings have such beings with them at all times. If humans realised this they may be able to communicate with them, and also all humans have Spirit Guides. In other words all humans have someone in spirit helping them without knowing. Many people today can and do relate to this Magnificent phenomena relating to other beings. Many people today speak to their spiritual guides every day. Many people will say to this 'what a lot of rubbish, that is not so'. Well to all of you who think that this is rubbish, sorry but not sorry, you are all definitely wrong. Most religions speak of Guardian Angels. Some have wings and some do not. Also many, many people verify this amazing gift in life every single day of the year. Not all people can see or hear their Spirit guides, but never the less, they all have them. Also many people love their life, so are not interested in spirituality at all, and then again those people are already in tune with their spiritual self. LOVE & LIGHT is who we all are, and that is a fact whether people believe it or not.

Once upon a time a certain gentleman

risked his life to save many others. Another being was trying his hardest to destroy. To all reading this story, which one, or which person has the right to do so? Also which person is wrong? In a spiritual realm all are correct except one is love and the other is not. Which person would you like to be? And that is how all of life is and that is a fact, believe it or not.

Many years ago a certain gentleman arrived at a certain land to realise that all was not the same around the world. When meeting people he realised a different tone and also a different language. A colour barrier was not necessary as all were smiling. This gentleman arrived on the shores after sailing around different parts of the mainland from where he was born. After many different methods of sign language he stayed at the leaders hut. During the night a mighty storm arrived and washed his vessel onto the rocks and was totally smashed beyond repair. In the morning many people helped this man with collecting all of his items of interest. This story relates to many others of similar experience. But the reason this story is written, is to tell and explain to all that beside language, colour, and attitude, everyone can and will one day live together in peace and harmony.

Many years ago another certain gentleman arrived at a certain land to realise that all was not the same around the world. This gentleman arrived with a group of people. Now a certain group, who thought that all of the existing people should be taught about life in a different manner. Well, according to most They had changed an entire country full of people. Now the same scenario, who is correct the one person or the group?.

Many years ago a certain group crucified a certain member of another group. The world understands the law of free will. Also the world and those who live upon it also understand, that what you do to others you do to yourself. Also the dark of night is required simply because of the sun, nothing more and nothing less. Now with this story, many people many years ago worshipped the night, but also ten times at least more people worshipped the sun. Now the moral of this story is that many people feel and think that the light and dark is equal. Actually that statement is untrue. Also this statement in spirituality is also untrue. The reason that most people think that way, do not actually know. They have been told, or that they have just read about it. In fact the ratio is commonly known by the spiritual realm as ninety two% light. Eight percent dark and that is a true fact.

Another once upon a time story. A certain gentleman called to the heaven's to ask for help with his injured wife.

The wife survived her injuries and her illness, just to get hit by a falling rock. This particular rock was dislodged by an earthquake. As she lay on the rubble her husband burst out crying and repeated his plea to the heavens. The lady in question passed into a coma and stopped breathing. With this her husband abused the heavens in a manner which he had never spoken before. The lady regained her consciousness, stood up and explained to the husband. I just went to the stars, it was so beautiful I did not choose to come back, but somebody said to me in a voice of pure love & light. "It, my dear, is not your time, back you go and also your husband loves you dearly."

Now to realise about this, it means that when your time is to return, that you do. And also to let everyone know reading this book, one does not return home until the exact time for them to do so. And also by the way, it is written in the Universal Scribes, when why and how you return. Love & light is who we all are and that is a fact, whether you believe it or not.

Now then, another time in life a gentleman helped with many lost soul's to return home. Also there were many others helping him. Now some certain groups of theology remain fixed that only good people go home. Other groups state that everyone goes home. And other groups just believe that nobody goes anywhere. Now a different group will say that there is only room in heaven for a very small number of well advanced souls. Now please excuse yourself if this is what you believe, for the true fact is, everybody goes to heaven. No one is excluded, and that is how life is. Everyone goes home. Now then, this story that was just written is in fact a true factual message relayed to those who are seeking the truth. This message has been relayed by Guides who are pure Love and Light and also work with the creator, who is pure Love and Light every moment of each moment. Now then, some people will disagree and that is also their right, but also there are many who agree, and then again how many books are there that have been written about this particular story. And therefore your belief is yours, There is a truth, so please find it if you choose to do so.

Once upon a time the message was given by the Creator of love & light to start a new energy of much higher vibration than ever before throughout the universe. The story that follows, is now the majority of beings can and do return home from whence they came. Now to continue with life itself. The people of the planet called earth continue to live as always except a little wiser spiritually. Several other galaxies with life existing also moved forward at a very fast rate. The slowest of all planets is the planet three steps below the planet earth. And just to let most people know who bother to read this book, that is so. Now the planet earth relies on Sun, Rain, Wind, and many other factors of creation. Many planets exist with life on them. Not only that but with intelligence far greater than the planet earth.

Now this story begins with a message to all.

LOVE & LIGHT IS WHO WE ALL ARE
LOVE & LIGHT IS ALL WE WILL EVER BE
LOVE& LIGHT IS WHAT THE CREATOR WAS, IS, AND WILL BE.

The other side of life is actually a myth, created by the creator for all to experience, and please remember all of this story is spiritual in reality.

Now reality is spiritual plus for a while physical. But as all know, spiritual beings are and will be always spiritual being's having an earthly experience. Once the physical has completed its soul's journey, the physical just decomposes into the ground to be part of the soil. Many people nowadays ask for the physical to be cremated, which is the burning of the physical body so that no part of the physical at all remains except ashes. Now many people say, ashes can be spread all over the ground if preferred, and that by doing so helps fertilise the ground. Many others claim to retain the ashes in what one calls an Urn. Now the spilling of ashes to some is an omen that the spirit is not happy with being in an Urn, also the spiritual self is trying to escape. Now To simplify all of these myths and theories, the spirit releases itself instantly from the body before the physical even finishes its physical time. And please remember, that these paragraphs in this book have been relayed to the author by those who are in spirit and from the highest realms of love & light. That is all regarding the physical body finishing its time on the earth plane.

John can be contacted on 61412926916

Queensland, Australia

EMAIL: johnwnant@optusnet.com.au

Printed in the United States
By Bookmasters